GENAI IN CLASSROOMS

Redefining Education in the
Post-Pandemic Era

Rakesh Kumar

*This book is humbly dedicated to Ishwar Chandra Vidyasagar
—a visionary educator, social reformer, and a true architect of
modern Indian education.*

*Born in an era when access to learning was a privilege of the
few, Vidyasagar stood as a beacon of progressive thought and
inclusive education. He championed the cause of women's
education, introduced rational reforms in the Bengali education
system, and worked relentlessly to make learning accessible
to the marginalized. At a time when rote learning and rigid
orthodoxy ruled the day, he advocated for critical thinking,
compassion, and the holistic development of the human mind.*

*Vidyasagar's efforts were not limited to curriculum reform
or institutional development. He fought societal dogmas,
translated classical texts into Bengali to democratize
knowledge, and stood fearlessly for justice and equality. His
work was rooted in empathy and powered by intellect—values
that align closely with the very ethos of this book.*

*As we now embrace Generative AI in classrooms, we walk a
path that Vidyasagar once paved with his pen, passion, and
principles. This book seeks to carry forward his legacy in a
digital age, where knowledge flows freely, inclusively, and
intelligently.*

*May the spirit of Ishwar Chandra Vidyasagar continue to inspire
educators, learners, and innovators across generations.*

CONTENTS

INTRODUCTION

The COVID-19 pandemic was not just a global health crisis—it was a major inflection point for the way we teach and learn. As classrooms emptied and screens replaced chalkboards, the world witnessed an overnight shift to digital education. This forced experiment with remote learning laid bare the strengths and weaknesses of traditional education systems, prompting a reevaluation of how knowledge is delivered, assessed, and personalized.

In the aftermath of this global disruption, a new wave of innovation has emerged at the intersection of education and technology. At the heart of this revolution is Generative Artificial Intelligence (GenAI)—a powerful set of tools that can generate human-like content, adapt to individual learning needs, and automate complex teaching tasks. GenAI isn't just enhancing education—it's redefining it.

This book explores the transformative potential of GenAI in modern classrooms. From personalized learning paths and real-time feedback systems to AI-assisted content creation and inclusive education strategies, we delve into how GenAI is reshaping the educational landscape. Drawing insights from global case studies, cutting-edge research, and the experiences of teachers and students, we examine how this technology is evolving from a futuristic concept into a practical classroom ally.

Whether you are an educator, policymaker, technologist, or

student, this book will guide you through the opportunities, challenges, ethics, and innovations of integrating GenAI into the world of education. Together, we will explore how to build an inclusive, accessible, and future-ready learning ecosystem—one where AI empowers humans, rather than replaces them.

Welcome to the classroom of the future.

THE CHANGING LANDSCAPE OF EDUCATION

Over the last decade, and especially after the COVID-19 pandemic, education has undergone a massive transformation —both in **delivery** and **design**. The traditional classroom model, with rows of desks, a blackboard, and face-to-face instruction, is no longer the only standard. Instead, the education sector has witnessed a shift toward **hybrid learning**, **remote education**, **digital tools**, and now the rise of **Generative AI (GenAI)**.

1. The Pandemic as a Catalyst

The global lockdowns of 2020 forced schools and universities to adopt online platforms almost overnight. Tools like Zoom, Google Classroom, and Microsoft Teams became virtual classrooms. Educators had to adapt quickly, and students had to shift their learning environments from classrooms to kitchen tables and bedrooms.

This sudden change exposed both the **strengths and weaknesses** of digital education:

- Strengths: Flexibility, accessibility, and scalability.
- Weaknesses: Digital divide, lack of engagement, and screen fatigue.

2. Digital Natives and Evolving Learner Expectations

Today's students are digital natives. They've grown up with smartphones, social media, and instant information. As a result:

- They expect **interactive**, **on-demand**, and **personalized** learning.
- Traditional one-size-fits-all methods are losing effectiveness.
- There's a demand for **engaging, multimedia-rich, and collaborative** educational experiences.

3. The Rise of EdTech and AI

The education technology industry exploded with innovations:

- Learning Management Systems (LMS)
- AI-powered tutoring
- Gamified learning apps
- Real-time assessments

Now, with **Generative AI**, we are entering a new frontier. AI can now:

- Generate quizzes instantly
- Create tailored lesson plans
- Explain complex topics in simple language
- Translate and transcribe in real-time
- Simulate conversations for language learning

4. Teachers as Facilitators, Not Sole Instructors

The teacher's role is evolving. No longer just dispensers of knowledge, teachers are becoming **facilitators**, **mentors**, and **co-learners**. With AI handling routine tasks, educators can now:

- Focus on creativity, empathy, and critical thinking
- Provide personalized support
- Engage more deeply with students

5. New Skills for a New Era

Education is also shifting from rote memorization to skills-based learning. Students need:

- Digital literacy
- AI awareness
- Critical thinking
- Emotional intelligence
- Collaboration in virtual teams

6. Equity, Accessibility & Inclusion

With AI and digital tools, there's an opportunity to:

- Provide **accessible learning** to students with disabilities
- Bring **quality education** to rural and underserved areas
- Translate content into local languages, breaking language barriers

Conclusion: A Landscape in Flux

The landscape of education is in a state of constant evolution —blending technology with tradition, and innovation with inclusion. As we move forward, **GenAI is poised to redefine not just how we teach, but how we learn, adapt, and grow**.

This moment isn't just about integrating tools—it's about **reimagining the purpose and potential of education** in the 21st century.

THE ROLE OF GENAI IN SHAPING THE FUTURE OF LEARNING

The future of learning is being rewritten—not just by technology, but by **Generative AI (GenAI)**. While traditional AI focused on automation and prediction, GenAI brings a creative, collaborative, and human-like intelligence to education. It doesn't just analyze; it *creates*. It doesn't just adapt; it *evolves* with the learner.

1. From Static Curriculum to Dynamic Content

In the past, educational content was largely static—textbooks, lesson plans, and videos designed for the average learner. With GenAI, the curriculum becomes **fluid and adaptive**:

- Lessons can be generated instantly based on a student's interest or comprehension level.
- Real-time content creation in multiple formats—text, video, images, even 3D simulations.
- Teachers can co-create content with GenAI, saving time while customizing for their students.

2. Personalized Learning at Scale

Every student learns differently. GenAI enables truly **personalized education**:

- Adaptive quizzes that adjust in real-time to student responses.

- Learning paths tailored to a student's pace, strengths, and weaknesses.
- Natural language interfaces that allow students to "talk" to an AI tutor anytime, anywhere.

3. 24/7 Intelligent Tutoring & Support

Imagine an AI tutor that never sleeps, never gets tired, and is available 24/7:

- GenAI can explain complex topics in simple terms—over and over, in different ways, until the student understands.
- It can offer examples, analogies, and explanations that match the student's learning style.
- It supports students outside of classroom hours—especially helpful in remote learning or for self-paced education.

4. Empowering Educators, Not Replacing Them

GenAI isn't here to replace teachers—it's here to **empower them**:

- Automating routine tasks like grading, content creation, and progress reports.
- Providing data insights into student performance and engagement.
- Enhancing lesson plans with creative input and global perspectives.

This allows educators to focus more on **mentorship, creativity, emotional intelligence, and critical thinking**—the human side of education.

5. Enhancing Collaboration and Communication

GenAI tools foster collaboration between:

- **Students and peers:** Through AI-assisted group projects and brainstorming.
- **Teachers and students:** With AI summarizing

discussions, managing queries, and tracking understanding.

- **Parents and educators:** With real-time updates on progress and personalized recommendations.

6. Breaking Language and Accessibility Barriers

Language is no longer a boundary:

- GenAI-powered translators and voice assistants allow real-time language support.
- Students with disabilities benefit from AI-generated closed captions, audio-to-text, text-to-speech, and more.
- Visual learners get infographics; auditory learners get spoken explanations—all generated on the fly.

7. Preparing Students for an AI-Driven World

By learning with GenAI, students aren't just learning academic content—they're gaining **AI fluency**, which will be critical in the coming decades. They are learning:

- How to interact with AI systems.
- How to question, challenge, and think critically about information.
- How to co-create with machines, not compete with them.

Conclusion: Learning Reimagined

GenAI is not a trend—it's a transformative force. It is reshaping classrooms, reimagining learning experiences, and realigning the roles of educators and learners. As we look to the future, the most impactful classrooms will be those that **embrace GenAI not just as a tool, but as a collaborator.**

We are not just preparing students for the future—we are **co-creating that future with them, through GenAI.**

WHAT IS GENAI?

Generative Artificial Intelligence (GenAI) is a branch of AI that goes beyond analyzing or processing information—it can **create** entirely new content. This includes:

- Text (like essays, emails, summaries)
- Images (like artwork, diagrams, or illustrations)
- Code (for websites or apps)
- Audio (like music or voice narration)
- Video (animations or simulations)

Unlike traditional AI, which follows strict patterns or rules, **GenAI learns from vast datasets and mimics creativity**, allowing it to generate responses, ideas, or outputs that feel human-like.

Simple Example of GenAI in Action (Education Setting)

Imagine a student in 8th grade struggling to understand **Photosynthesis**.

With GenAI:

- The student asks, *"Can you explain photosynthesis to me like I'm 10 years old?"*
- GenAI responds with:

"Photosynthesis is like a cooking process that plants do using sunlight. They take water from the ground and carbon dioxide from the air and, using sunlight, turn it into food for themselves and oxygen for us!"

If the student wants:

- **A diagram** → GenAI can draw or generate one.
- **A quiz** → GenAI can instantly make practice questions.
- **A story format** → GenAI can explain it through a fun story about a leaf going on a food-making adventure!

Why is GenAI Revolutionary in Education?

- It can **personalize** learning based on a student's level.
- It offers **instant help**, anytime.
- It makes lessons more **engaging** with stories, visuals, and interactive elements.
- It helps teachers by **automating content creation** and assessments.

Real-World Tools Using GenAI

- **ChatGPT**: Answers questions, helps with homework, writes summaries.
- **Khanmigo** (by Khan Academy): An AI tutor powered by GPT.
- **DALL·E**: Creates images from text prompts for use in lessons or activities.

In Summary:

GenAI = An AI that Creates.

It's not just smart—it's *imaginative*, *interactive*, and *educational*. In classrooms, it's like having a **digital co-teacher, tutor, and content creator—all rolled into one.**

A BRIEF HISTORY OF AI IN EDUCATION

Artificial Intelligence (AI) and education have been connected for decades—but the journey has evolved significantly over time. From rule-based tutoring systems to adaptive learning platforms and now to **Generative AI**, AI's influence has reshaped the way we teach and learn.

1. The Beginnings (1960s–1980s): Rule-Based Systems

AI's role in education began with **intelligent tutoring systems (ITS)**.

- Early systems like **SCHOLAR** and **PLATO** used simple if-then logic to guide students through basic subjects like geography and mathematics.
- These systems followed rigid rules and couldn't adapt much to different learning styles.
- Despite their limitations, they showed that **machines could guide learning**, even in a basic form.

2. The Rise of Adaptive Learning (1990s–2000s)

With the growth of computing power, AI systems became more dynamic:

- AI-powered platforms like **Cognitive Tutors** were introduced. These could:
  - Track a student's progress,
  - Adjust the difficulty of questions,

- ○ Provide personalized feedback.
- The concept of **"learning analytics"** began to emerge—AI started to collect and analyze student performance data to support teachers.

3. The EdTech Boom (2010s): Personalized Learning Goes Mainstream

The 2010s saw the explosion of EdTech tools using AI, thanks to cloud computing and big data:

- Platforms like **Khan Academy**, **Coursera**, and **Duolingo** integrated AI to personalize content and keep learners engaged.
- AI was used to:
  - ○ Recommend topics,
  - ○ Create learning paths,
  - ○ Automate assessments and grading.
- Chatbots began to assist with answering questions and providing help.

4. AI Meets the Classroom (Mid-2010s–2020): Early Classroom Integration

- AI was slowly adopted in classrooms for administrative tasks:
  - ○ Grading essays,
  - ○ Monitoring attendance,
  - ○ Flagging students at risk of falling behind.
- Smart content tools were introduced—like AI that could generate **practice questions**, **flashcards**, or **lesson summaries**.
- However, AI still played a **supportive role**—not a central one.

5. Post-Pandemic Acceleration (2020–2022): Urgency Meets

Innovation

The COVID-19 pandemic forced global education online—**accelerating the adoption of AI tools**:

- Teachers turned to AI-driven tools for lesson delivery, classroom management, and engagement.
- Platforms like **Google Classroom, Zoom with AI captioning**, and **Microsoft Teams** became essential.
- The gap in **digital literacy** and **access** became more visible, highlighting the need for scalable AI-powered education.

6. The GenAI Revolution (2023–Present): Creativity and Conversation

Enter **Generative AI (GenAI)**—a game-changer in education.

- Tools like **ChatGPT, Bard, Claude, and DALL·E** can:
  - Write essays,
  - Summarize textbooks,
  - Generate teaching materials,
  - Explain concepts interactively,
  - Create visuals, quizzes, and even videos.
- Now, students can chat with AI tutors anytime, and teachers can design an entire curriculum in minutes with GenAI support.

In Summary:

The role of AI in education has evolved from:

Rule-based tutoring → Adaptive learning → Predictive analytics → Generative content creation.

We're entering a time when AI isn't just enhancing education—it's **redefining it**.

THE PANDEMIC'S IMPACT ON EDUCATION: A TURNING POINT

The COVID-19 pandemic didn't just disrupt education—it **transformed it**. What began as a global crisis became a critical **turning point** that exposed long-standing issues, accelerated digital adoption, and opened the doors to new technologies like **Generative AI**.

1. Disruption of Traditional Learning

- In early 2020, schools and universities across the world were forced to shut down.
- Over **1.6 billion students** were affected globally.
- Chalkboards and physical classrooms were replaced by **Zoom**, **Google Meet**, and **learning management systems** (LMS).

This abrupt shift from in-person to remote learning revealed just how **unprepared** the global education system was for digital instruction.

2. Exposure of Inequities

- Students from underserved communities lacked access to:

- ○ Devices (laptops, tablets)
- ○ High-speed internet
- ○ Safe and quiet learning environments
- The **digital divide** widened existing educational gaps, making equity a global concern.

3. The Rise of EdTech and Online Learning Tools

- EdTech platforms like **Khan Academy, Byju's, Coursera**, and **edX** saw massive growth.
- Teachers and students quickly adopted tools like:
  - ○ Digital whiteboards
  - ○ Automated quizzes
  - ○ Cloud-based collaboration tools
- Learning moved to **asynchronous and hybrid models**, breaking the boundaries of the classroom.

4. Mental Health and Engagement Challenges

- Students faced **isolation, anxiety, and burnout** from extended screen time and lack of social interaction.
- Teachers struggled to keep learners **motivated and engaged** through digital means alone.
- This led to a call for **more humanized technology—** tools that could simulate interaction, empathy, and creativity.

5. Catalyst for Innovation and Flexibility

- Educational institutions began to **experiment and innovate**:
  - ○ Flipped classrooms
  - ○ Micro-learning modules
  - ○ Virtual reality (VR) and AI-based assessments
- Governments and educators realized that **flexibility**

was no longer optional—it was essential.

6. The Entry of AI & GenAI into Classrooms

- As the demand for personalized and scalable education grew, **AI stepped in**.
- Post-pandemic, **Generative AI** emerged as a solution to:
  - Personalize learning at scale
  - Automate lesson and content creation
  - Provide 24/7 tutoring and assistance
- Teachers began to explore AI as a **collaborator** rather than a tool.

In Summary:

The pandemic was a **reset button** for education. It forced the world to rethink:

What is essential? Who is being left behind? How can we make learning more flexible, inclusive, and future-ready?

And most importantly—**how can technology like GenAI help us build a better educational system for all?**

WHY GENAI IS THE KEY TO POST-PANDEMIC EDUCATIONAL TRANSFORMATION

The pandemic didn't just disrupt education—it **exposed its vulnerabilities** and revealed the urgent need for a more adaptable, inclusive, and personalized learning system. As schools and educators seek lasting solutions in this new era, **Generative AI (GenAI)** emerges not as a temporary fix, but as the **transformative engine** of 21st-century education.

1. Personalized Learning at Scale

Every student learns differently. GenAI can:

- Tailor explanations based on individual learning styles (visual, auditory, kinesthetic).
- Adjust difficulty levels in real time.
- Create personalized quizzes, summaries, and flashcards.

For example, if a student struggles with algebra, GenAI can generate simpler analogies and practice problems—instantly.

2. 24/7 Tutoring and On-Demand Support

GenAI-based tools like ChatGPT provide round-the-clock assistance:

- Answering student queries.
- Explaining complex topics in plain language.
- Providing step-by-step guidance.

This reduces dependence on classroom time alone and ensures students don't feel left behind.

3. Empowering Educators, Not Replacing Them

Teachers remain the heart of education. GenAI:

- Assists in lesson planning and content creation.
- Designs interactive activities or assessments in seconds.
- Suggests differentiated materials for mixed-ability classrooms.

With GenAI handling routine tasks, teachers can focus more on mentoring, emotional support, and classroom engagement.

4. Bridging Learning Gaps

The pandemic deepened educational inequality. GenAI helps bridge these gaps by:

- Offering multilingual support and translations.
- Simplifying content for students with learning disabilities.
- Supporting remote learners with adaptive content delivery.

A student in a rural area with limited resources can now access the same quality support as one in a top-tier urban school.

5. Encouraging Creativity and Exploration

GenAI isn't just for solving math problems—it can:

- Co-create stories with students.
- Generate science experiments.
- Help design digital art or music projects.

It transforms passive learning into **creative exploration**, making education more engaging and joyful.

6. Supporting a Hybrid and Future-Ready Education Model

Post-pandemic learning is no longer bound to four walls. GenAI enables:

- Seamless hybrid and flipped classrooms.
- Smart content generation for both online and offline delivery.
- Integration with LMS platforms, VR, AR, and digital labs.

This flexibility ensures education continues—even amid future disruptions.

In Summary:

GenAI is not just a tool—it's a learning partner.

It brings **equity, flexibility, creativity**, and **scalability** to education in ways that traditional models cannot. In the post-pandemic world, GenAI stands at the center of a **more resilient, human-centered, and intelligent educational ecosystem.**

REMOTE LEARNING: THE PANDEMIC ERA'S FORCED EXPERIMENT

When the COVID-19 pandemic swept across the globe in early 2020, traditional education systems were faced with an unprecedented challenge: **how to continue learning when schools and universities had to shut their doors**. What followed was an **instant, global experiment in remote learning**—one that, while born out of necessity, would forever change the future of education.

---

1. The Sudden Shift to Online Learning

- In a matter of weeks, over **1.6 billion students** worldwide transitioned from in-person classes to **remote learning**.
- Educational institutions scrambled to move lessons, assessments, and even social interaction online.
- Platforms like **Zoom**, **Google Meet**, **Microsoft Teams**, and **Skype** became the primary tools for classroom interaction.

The move from face-to-face to virtual learning was **unplanned**, untested, and, for many, overwhelming.

---

2. The Immediate Challenges of Remote Learning

While the shift was necessary, it highlighted numerous

challenges:

- **Technology Gaps:** Not all students had access to reliable internet or devices. Rural areas, low-income families, and developing countries struggled with these disparities.

- **Teacher Training:** Many educators were not prepared to teach online. They had little experience with digital teaching tools or remote classroom management.

- **Student Engagement:** Without physical presence, students found it difficult to stay focused, motivated, and engaged.

- **Emotional Impact:** Remote learning lacked the **social interactions** students are accustomed to, leading to feelings of isolation and burnout.

As a result, remote learning was not a perfect solution—it was a **forced experiment**, with mixed results.

3. The Silver Lining: Opportunities for Innovation

Despite the hurdles, the pandemic also accelerated **innovation** and **adoption of technology** in education:

- **EdTech Adoption:** The use of educational technologies exploded. Platforms like **Khan Academy**, **Duolingo**, **Coursera**, and **Byju's** became essential to ensure continuity in education.

- **Learning Management Systems (LMS):** Schools adopted platforms such as **Google Classroom**, **Moodle**, and **Blackboard**, allowing teachers to organize lessons, share resources, and track progress.

- **Increased Flexibility:** Remote learning introduced more flexible schedules, allowing students to learn at their own pace and access content from anywhere.

- **Personalized Learning:** Tools like **AI-powered tutors** and **adaptive learning technologies** began to gain traction, offering more customized learning experiences.

In many ways, the **forced experiment** laid the groundwork for a **future of education** that embraces both physical and virtual learning environments.

4. The Rise of Hybrid Learning Models

As schools began to re-open, many didn't fully return to traditional methods. Instead, **hybrid learning models** emerged:

- **Blended classrooms** combined in-person and online elements, where students could attend physical classes while also accessing digital content and interacting with online peers.
- **Flipped classrooms** became more common, where students learned the content at home through videos and materials, and class time was dedicated to discussions, projects, or application of concepts.

These models allowed for **greater flexibility** and more personalized learning, providing benefits from both traditional and remote settings.

5. Remote Learning and the Future: A New Educational Paradigm

While the immediate future of education post-pandemic remains uncertain, the lessons learned from remote learning have paved the way for a **new paradigm** in education:

- **Increased Access to Education:** Remote learning technologies have enabled access to quality education for students in remote or underserved areas.
- **Global Collaboration:** Students and teachers can now collaborate with peers from around the world, thanks to virtual platforms.

- **Lifelong Learning:** The shift to online learning has created opportunities for **adult education, upskilling,** and **reskilling** as a lifelong pursuit, without geographical barriers.

Remote learning was not just an emergency solution—it has **redefined the possibilities** of what education can be in the 21st century.

In Summary:

The pandemic forced a global shift to remote learning, presenting both significant challenges and **incredible opportunities**. It wasn't an ideal experiment, but it allowed education systems to **test the limits of technology** and **reimagine** what the future of learning could look like—**flexible, digital, and more accessible** than ever before.

HYBRID LEARNING: BLENDING THE BEST OF BOTH WORLDS

As educational institutions navigate the post-pandemic world, **hybrid learning** has emerged as one of the most promising models to **combine the best of traditional in-person education** with the **flexibility and innovation of online learning**. This model, which combines **face-to-face** instruction with **digital tools** and **online resources**, offers a more **personalized** and **inclusive** learning experience.

1. Defining Hybrid Learning

Hybrid learning refers to an **educational model** that blends:

- **In-person instruction**: Traditional classroom teaching where teachers and students interact face-to-face.
- **Online learning**: Digital platforms, such as Learning Management Systems (LMS), video conferencing, and AI-driven tools, that support flexible, remote learning.

The key to hybrid learning is its **flexibility**—students can attend classes physically, but they also have the option to participate virtually or asynchronously.

2. The Benefits of Hybrid Learning

A. Flexibility and Convenience

- Students can choose to attend classes **in-person** or

online depending on their schedules, health concerns, or learning preferences.

- **Recorded lessons** and resources are available to students who may have missed a class, allowing them to learn at their own pace.

For example, students who have a **family emergency** or live in remote areas can still continue their education without disruption.

B. Increased Engagement and Interactivity

- Hybrid learning allows for a more **dynamic learning experience**:
  - **In-class activities** can be complemented by **online discussions**, collaborative projects, and access to **digital resources**.
  - Teachers can leverage digital tools for instant quizzes, feedback, and interactive content.

Interactive elements like **polls**, **real-time discussions**, and **group work via virtual platforms** keep students engaged, even in virtual settings.

C. Personalized Learning at Scale

- Hybrid classrooms allow educators to cater to different learning styles:
  - **Visual learners** can benefit from digital content like videos and simulations.
  - **Auditory learners** can participate in virtual lectures, podcasts, or voice-guided tutorials.
  - **Kinesthetic learners** can work on hands-on projects in the classroom and then follow up with digital resources.

GenAI can further personalize learning by **adapting content** to individual student needs, ensuring that every learner can progress at their own pace.

D. Broader Access and Inclusivity

- Hybrid learning breaks down barriers for **students with disabilities**, those living in rural areas, or those with limited access to physical classrooms.
- **Special accommodations** such as **closed captioning**, **screen readers**, or **alternative assessments** can be seamlessly integrated into hybrid systems.

Hybrid learning allows for a **more inclusive education system** where every student, regardless of background or ability, has the opportunity to thrive.

3. Key Elements of Successful Hybrid Learning

To effectively implement hybrid learning, certain elements must be in place:

A. Robust Digital Infrastructure

- **Reliable internet access** and **devices** are essential to ensure equal participation in the learning process.
- Institutions must invest in Learning Management Systems (LMS) and collaboration tools (e.g., **Zoom**, **Google Meet**, **Microsoft Teams**) that can support both in-person and remote interactions.

B. Integrated Learning Tools

- Hybrid learning requires a **well-coordinated system** where digital tools (like **GenAI platforms**, **virtual labs**, **online quizzes**) are integrated seamlessly into the classroom.
- Teachers need to be trained on how to use **online platforms** for delivering content, creating assessments, and providing feedback.

C. Clear Communication and Structure

- Students and teachers must understand the **hybrid model's expectations**:
  - When to attend in-person sessions.

- How to engage in virtual learning.
- Deadlines and responsibilities for both modes.

GenAI can also help by providing **intelligent scheduling**, **automated reminders**, and **learning progress tracking** for students.

4. GenAI's Role in Hybrid Learning

In a hybrid learning environment, **Generative AI (GenAI)** can be an essential tool for maximizing the learning experience:

A. Personalized Content Creation

- GenAI can **generate customized study materials**, such as practice questions, study guides, and summaries, based on a student's progress and needs.
- It can automatically adjust the **difficulty level** of exercises or **recommend supplementary resources** based on the student's performance.

B. Real-Time Feedback and Assessment

- AI-driven systems can analyze student work and provide **instant feedback**, whether it's a quiz, written assignment, or project.
- GenAI can also help teachers by **automating assessments** and flagging areas where students need extra help.

C. Enhanced Communication

- Virtual assistants powered by **GenAI** can answer common student queries, guide them through course content, and provide **24/7 support**.

This allows for **continuous learning**, even outside traditional classroom hours, fostering greater independence and self-direction in students.

5. Challenges and Considerations

While hybrid learning presents many advantages, it also poses certain challenges:

A. Technological Barriers

- Not all students may have access to the technology required for hybrid learning. Schools must address the **digital divide** by ensuring equitable access to devices and high-speed internet.

B. Teacher Training and Preparedness

- Educators need adequate training in using digital tools and platforms to manage hybrid classrooms effectively.

C. Student Motivation

- With the option to attend virtually, some students may struggle with **self-discipline** and **engagement**. Continuous effort is required to motivate and support them.

Effective integration of **GenAI** can help mitigate these challenges by providing **personalized guidance**, engaging content, and constant feedback to keep students on track.

In Summary:

Hybrid learning represents a **flexible, inclusive, and future-ready approach** to education, combining the best of both in-person and online learning. It offers **personalized experiences**, enhances engagement, and breaks down barriers to learning. With the support of **GenAI**, hybrid learning becomes even more powerful, enabling students to learn at their own pace and ensuring that education remains accessible, relevant, and innovative.

THE RISE OF ONLINE CLASSROOMS AND DIGITAL PLATFORMS

The COVID-19 pandemic forced the world to pivot rapidly from traditional classroom setups to **online learning environments**. While initially a stopgap solution, this shift triggered a digital revolution in education, accelerating the development and adoption of **online classrooms** and **digital learning platforms** on an unprecedented scale. What started as a necessity quickly evolved into a powerful alternative — and in many cases, a **complement — to traditional education**.

1. The Catalyst: A Global Shift to Remote Learning

When schools and universities were shut down to curb the spread of COVID-19, **online classrooms became the primary mode of instruction**. This urgent need sparked innovation and investment in:

- Video conferencing tools (e.g., **Zoom, Google Meet, Microsoft Teams**)
- Learning Management Systems (LMS) like **Moodle, Canvas**, and **Blackboard**
- Content-sharing platforms like **Khan Academy, Coursera, edX**, and **YouTube**

Suddenly, millions of students were **logging in from home**, and teachers had to **reimagine their pedagogy for digital delivery**.

2. Features of Online Classrooms

Digital classrooms redefined the learning experience with several innovative features:

- **Live sessions** with screen sharing and breakout rooms
- **Asynchronous content** (pre-recorded videos, readings, and assignments)
- **Automated grading** and instant quizzes
- **Discussion forums** and collaboration tools
- **Data analytics** for tracking student progress

These tools created **interactive, flexible, and personalized** learning environments — something traditional classrooms often struggled to provide at scale.

3. Digital Platforms: Enablers of Scalable Education

Digital education platforms became the backbone of this transformation:

- **Khan Academy** offered free, curriculum-aligned content globally.
- **Coursera** and **edX** democratized access to university-level courses.
- **Byju's**, **Unacademy**, and similar platforms flourished in countries like India, offering localized, high-quality content.

These platforms empowered educators to **reach thousands —even millions—of learners**, breaking geographical and economic barriers.

4. GenAI's Entry into Digital Learning

The recent wave of **Generative AI** tools further advanced online education:

- **ChatGPT** became a personal tutor, capable of

explaining topics, summarizing texts, and generating quizzes.

- Platforms like **Khanmigo (Khan Academy's GenAI tool)** offered personalized help using AI.

- **AI-driven feedback** on writing, code, or mathematical problems allowed for instant learning loops.

GenAI made digital learning **more adaptive, interactive, and context-aware**—a huge leap from static online content.

5. Advantages of Online Classrooms and Platforms

- **Accessibility**: Students can learn anytime, anywhere.

- **Affordability**: Many platforms offer free or low-cost education.

- **Scalability**: One teacher can reach thousands of students.

- **Customization**: GenAI enables tailored content for each learner's pace and style.

- **Continuous learning**: Learners can revisit material, practice, and get feedback instantly.

6. Challenges and Considerations

Despite the benefits, online learning also comes with challenges:

- **Digital Divide**: Not all students have access to devices and high-speed internet.

- **Lack of Social Interaction**: Physical classrooms offer interpersonal development that is hard to replicate online.

- **Motivation and Discipline**: Self-paced learning demands strong personal drive, which not all learners possess.

Solutions lie in **hybrid learning, policy-level changes**, and **technological support systems** — all enhanced by GenAI capabilities.

In Summary:

The rise of online classrooms and digital platforms marked a **transformational moment in the history of education**. These platforms are now central to the modern learning ecosystem, enabling personalized, scalable, and inclusive education. With **GenAI stepping in as an intelligent companion**, online education is not just a temporary fix—it's an integral part of education's future.

CHALLENGES FACED BY STUDENTS AND EDUCATORS IN THE PANDEMIC ERA

The COVID-19 pandemic abruptly transformed the global education landscape, pushing millions of students and educators into uncharted digital territories. While this sudden shift accelerated the adoption of online learning and opened new possibilities, it also brought forth a wide range of challenges—technological, emotional, social, and pedagogical.

1. Digital Divide: Unequal Access to Technology

Not all students and educators had equal access to:

- **Reliable internet connectivity**
- **Laptops, tablets, or smartphones**
- **Quiet, dedicated spaces for learning or teaching**

This **inequality in access** created significant gaps in participation, especially among students in rural areas or underprivileged communities.

Example: In many countries, millions of students went completely offline due to lack of digital resources.

2. Mental Health and Emotional Strain

Both students and teachers experienced:

- **Isolation and loneliness**
- **Anxiety over academic performance or job security**
- **Burnout due to extended screen time and blurred work-life boundaries**

Many schools reported an increase in **depression, stress, and disengagement**.

3. Lack of Preparedness Among Educators

Most teachers were **not trained** for digital pedagogy. Challenges included:

- Learning new tools like Zoom, Google Classroom, etc.
- Redesigning lesson plans for online formats
- Managing **virtual discipline** and student engagement

Educators had to **upskill overnight**, often with little institutional support.

4. Engagement and Attention Issues

Online classes often failed to:

- Capture student attention effectively
- Facilitate meaningful discussions
- Maintain motivation and consistent attendance

Distractions at home, combined with screen fatigue, led to **low retention and comprehension** rates.

5. Assessment and Academic Integrity

Conducting fair and effective assessments was another challenge:

- Increased cases of **cheating and plagiarism**
- Lack of proper **proctoring tools**

- Difficulty in evaluating **soft skills** like collaboration or communication

Teachers struggled to balance **rigor with empathy** during grading.

6. Special Needs and Younger Learners

Students with learning disabilities or those in early education faced:

- Difficulties adapting to virtual learning
- Lack of personalized, hands-on support
- Reduced social interaction and physical activity

Parents were often required to **step in as co-educators**, which wasn't feasible for all families.

7. Curriculum and Content Delivery Gaps

The sudden shift often led to:

- Incomplete syllabi
- Over-reliance on lecture-based formats
- Limited experiential or lab-based learning

Subjects requiring physical demonstration, like science labs or arts, suffered heavily.

8. Cultural and Language Barriers

For international schools and diverse regions, challenges included:

- Adapting content for **multilingual** classrooms
- Bridging **cultural expectations** in digital settings
- Managing students from **different time zones**

In Summary:

The pandemic-era education system highlighted **deep-rooted structural and technological issues**. Both students and teachers faced immense pressure to adapt, often with limited resources and guidance. These challenges revealed the **urgent need for innovation, inclusivity, mental health support**, and **technology-enhanced resilience** in educational systems.

WHAT IS PERSONALIZED LEARNING?

Personalized Learning is an educational approach that tailors learning experiences to meet the **unique needs, preferences, abilities, and interests** of each student. Rather than following a one-size-fits-all model, personalized learning allows students to progress at their own pace, use preferred learning methods, and explore subjects that resonate with their goals and passions.

At its core, personalized learning recognizes that **every student learns differently**, and it leverages technology, data, and sometimes AI (like GenAI) to **optimize learning paths for individuals**.

Key Features of Personalized Learning

1. **Student-Centered Approach**
   - Focuses on the learner's strengths, weaknesses, and interests.
   - Empowers students to take ownership of their learning journey.

2. **Paced to the Learner**
   - Students move forward when they **master a concept**, not just because the class moves on.
   - This **flexibility** helps avoid both boredom and overwhelm.

3. **Customized Learning Paths**
   - Content, tools, and assessments are **adapted** to suit each learner's level.
   - Examples include learning playlists, adaptive learning software, or AI-generated quizzes.

4. **Frequent Feedback and Data-Driven Adjustments**
   - Teachers and systems use **real-time data** to update content and strategies.
   - Allows timely **intervention** and support.

5. **Multiple Modes of Instruction**
   - Learning materials may be delivered through **videos, texts, games, simulations, or chatbots**.
   - Students can choose how they best absorb information.

How GenAI Powers Personalized Learning

GenAI takes personalized learning to the next level by:

- Generating **instant explanations**, examples, and summaries based on a student's questions.
- Creating **custom quizzes, learning plans, or assignments**.
- Acting as a **24/7 tutor**, answering queries in natural language.
- Recommending **learning resources** tailored to a student's performance and interests.

Example: A 10th-grade student struggling with algebra can ask a GenAI tool like ChatGPT to explain a concept in simple terms, show step-by-step solutions, or even generate practice problems based on their learning level.

Why Personalized Learning Matters in the Post-Pandemic Era

- Students returned to school with **learning gaps** caused by disrupted education.

- One-size-fits-all models are **ineffective** in addressing those gaps.

- Personalized learning enables **recovery and acceleration**, giving each student a fair chance to succeed.

- GenAI helps teachers **scale personalization**, making it feasible for classrooms of all sizes.

In Summary:

Personalized learning is about **meeting each student where they are**—intellectually, emotionally, and academically. With GenAI, what once seemed like a futuristic ideal is now a **practical reality**, reshaping how knowledge is delivered and how success is achieved in modern education.

ADAPTIVE LEARNING SYSTEMS POWERED BY GENAI

As classrooms evolve in the post-pandemic world, the need for **personalized, flexible, and responsive education** has never been greater. This is where **Adaptive Learning Systems**, supercharged by **Generative AI (GenAI)**, step in to revolutionize the learning experience.

What is an Adaptive Learning System?

An **Adaptive Learning System** is a technology-based platform that continuously adjusts the way content is delivered based on a learner's:

- **Performance**
- **Learning style**
- **Pace**
- **Knowledge gaps**

Instead of a static curriculum, these systems **"learn" from the learner**, offering **real-time adaptations** to optimize comprehension and engagement.

Think of it as a smart tutor that evolves with the student.

How GenAI Enhances Adaptive Learning

While traditional adaptive systems rely on data-driven

algorithms, **GenAI brings a new level of intelligence, creativity, and interaction** to the mix.

1. Dynamic Content Generation

GenAI can:

- Generate **custom questions, explanations, summaries, and practice problems** based on a student's current performance.
- Adjust the **tone, complexity, and format** of learning materials in real-time.

2. Conversational Interactions

- Learners can engage with GenAI chatbots that behave like **virtual tutors**, available 24/7.
- These bots answer questions, correct misconceptions, and even provide **emotional support**.

3. Cognitive Pattern Recognition

GenAI analyzes how students respond and identifies:

- Confusion patterns
- Confidence levels
- Fatigue or disengagement signals
  It then **tailors the next steps** accordingly.

4. Smart Assessments

- GenAI can craft **adaptive quizzes** that get harder or easier based on real-time answers.
- It evaluates open-ended responses, giving **instant feedback** and even suggestions for improvement.

5. Multimodal Learning Paths

- Generates content in various formats (videos, text, simulations, voice, etc.) to suit **different learning styles**.
- Supports students with special needs or

language barriers through **accessibility-focused customization**.

Example: Adaptive Learning with GenAI in Action

Let's say a high school student named Priya is learning algebra.

1. She logs into a GenAI-powered platform.
2. Based on her performance history, it starts her with basic linear equations.
3. As she progresses, it notices she struggles with word problems.
4. GenAI generates simpler versions of those problems and explains the logic step-by-step.
5. It shifts the instruction into **interactive dialogue**, asking her questions in a conversational format.
6. Priya chooses to see a **visual explainer video**, also generated by GenAI.
7. After improvement, the system challenges her with higher-order problems and tracks her progress.

Benefits of GenAI-Driven Adaptive Learning

Benefit	Description
Precision Targeting	Addresses specific learner weaknesses instantly
Time Efficiency	Saves time by focusing only on what the student needs
Interactive Learning	Makes learning engaging through natural conversation
Teacher Support	Provides insights and data to help teachers intervene
Scalability	Works across languages, subjects,

and regions

In Summary:

Adaptive learning systems powered by GenAI represent a **paradigm shift in education**—moving from reactive to proactive, from general to personal. These systems make education more **inclusive, effective, and engaging**, especially in a world where students are more diverse and distributed than ever before.

HOW GENAI TAILORS EDUCATIONAL CONTENT TO INDIVIDUAL NEEDS

In the era of digital learning, **one-size-fits-all education** is no longer sufficient. Students have diverse abilities, interests, learning speeds, and comprehension styles. **Generative AI (GenAI)** plays a transformative role in making education more **personalized, adaptive, and impactful** by tailoring content to the unique needs of each learner.

What Does "Tailoring Educational Content" Mean?

Tailoring means:

- Modifying the **delivery, depth**, and **format** of content
- Aligning lessons with the **learner's goals, skill levels, and preferences**
- Adjusting content dynamically based on **student interaction and feedback**

It is essentially **smart customization** that makes learning more relevant and effective.

How GenAI Makes Personalization Possible

1. Real-Time Data Analysis

GenAI analyzes:

- Student performance
- Behavior patterns
- Preferred learning modes
  It uses this data to **adapt content instantly**—whether by changing the difficulty, explanation method, or type of activity.

2. Dynamic Content Generation

GenAI can:

- Generate practice problems tailored to current skill level
- Provide simpler or more advanced versions of the same concept
- Offer explanations in multiple formats (text, video, diagrams)

Example: A student struggling with photosynthesis can ask the GenAI to explain it "like I'm in 5th grade" or "using a real-life analogy."

3. Learning Style Adaptation

GenAI identifies if a student learns best through:

- Visual content (diagrams, infographics)
- Auditory means (narration, podcasts)
- Kinesthetic interaction (games, simulations)
  Then it **delivers the content accordingly**.

4. Goal-Oriented Learning Paths

Whether the student is preparing for an exam, catching up after an absence, or exploring a passion topic, GenAI **builds a custom learning track** that aligns with specific outcomes.

5. Language and Accessibility Adjustments

GenAI can:

- Translate content to the learner's native language
- Adjust complexity for different reading levels
- Add closed captions, narration, or dyslexia-friendly fonts

Personalization in Action: A Scenario

Imagine a GenAI-powered classroom platform:

- **Ananya**, a 9th-grade student, logs in and says, "I'm struggling with quadratic equations."
- The system:
  - Scans her recent quizzes and notes where she made mistakes
  - Generates a set of beginner-friendly examples
  - Offers a short explainer video and interactive graphing activity
  - Follows up with a short quiz tailored to her weaknesses
  - As she improves, the difficulty automatically increases

All of this happens in minutes—**no waiting for the teacher or fixed schedules.**

Key Benefits

Feature	Benefit
Custom content	Keeps learners engaged and challenged at the right level
Progress-based pacing	Ensures mastery before moving forward
Inclusivity	Supports diverse learners and learning needs
Empowerment	Builds student confidence and ownership

The Teacher's Role

GenAI doesn't replace teachers—it **augments** them:

- Frees up time for teachers to focus on mentorship and creativity
- Provides data and insights on student progress
- Suggests interventions or support strategies when needed

In Summary

GenAI tailors educational content by continuously learning about the learner and adjusting materials to fit their unique needs. This personalized experience not only improves academic performance but also nurtures a deeper love for learning. It's a powerful step toward making **education truly student-centered** in the post-pandemic, tech-driven world.

CASE STUDIES OF GENAI IN PERSONALIZED LEARNING

As GenAI continues to reshape education, real-world implementations offer powerful insights into its effectiveness. These **case studies** demonstrate how educational institutions, platforms, and classrooms are leveraging GenAI to **deliver personalized learning experiences** and transform educational outcomes.

Case Study 1: Squirrel AI – Personalized Learning in China

Background:
Squirrel AI is an adaptive learning company in China that uses AI, including GenAI components, to deliver **individualized tutoring** in K–12 education.

How GenAI Helped:

- Students take diagnostic assessments to identify knowledge gaps.
- GenAI algorithms tailor lesson plans to the exact needs of each student.
- The system generates **real-time feedback**, suggests remedial material, and adapts questions based on performance.

Impact:

- Students using Squirrel AI outperformed their peers by **20%** in national test scores.
- Teachers reported a significant reduction in workload due to AI's automatic grading and lesson planning.

Case Study 2: Khanmigo by Khan Academy – AI as a Personal Tutor

Background:

Khan Academy, a well-known global learning platform, introduced **Khanmigo**, a GenAI-powered assistant using GPT technology.

How GenAI Helped:

- Acts as a **conversational tutor**, answering questions, guiding problem-solving, and explaining concepts.
- Adapts tone and complexity based on age and understanding.
- Supports both students and teachers with tailored explanations and resource suggestions.

Impact:

- Students reported **increased confidence** in difficult subjects like math and science.
- Teachers used Khanmigo to **differentiate instruction** in large classrooms, reaching both advanced learners and those needing support.

Case Study 3: OpenStax Tutor – Tailored College-Level Learning

Background:

Rice University's **OpenStax Tutor** is an AI-powered platform designed for college students.

How GenAI Helped:

- Tracks student interactions to understand knowledge retention.
- Generates **custom quizzes, flashcards, and explanations** based on performance.
- Delivers material in a format best suited to the learner's preferences (text, visuals, examples).

Impact:

- Students using the system showed **higher engagement and grades**.
- It enabled **independent learning**, especially beneficial for online or remote students.

Case Study 4: India's AI-Based EdTech Startups (e.g., Embibe)

Background:
Platforms like **Embibe** use GenAI to assist Indian students preparing for competitive exams such as JEE, NEET, and UPSC.

How GenAI Helped:

- Conducts deep analysis of student performance.
- Generates **personalized improvement plans**.
- Offers **confidence-building feedback** and targeted practice materials.

Impact:

- Over 70% of students using Embibe reported improved performance.
- Reduced student anxiety by giving **clear learning paths and motivational nudges**.

Case Study 5: Virtual GenAI Classrooms in the UAE

Background:
Schools in the UAE integrated GenAI-powered classroom tools to address **learning gaps caused by the pandemic**.

How GenAI Helped:

- Delivered real-time, adaptive lessons to hybrid learners.
- Offered **instant explanations and re-teaching strategies** when students showed confusion.
- Enabled students to explore topics **beyond the standard curriculum**.

Impact:

- Teachers noted a 40% improvement in student participation.
- Students expressed feeling more **in control of their learning journeys**.

Key Takeaways Across Case Studies

Feature	Benefit
Targeted Interventions	Students receive help exactly where needed
Real-Time Support	No delay in feedback or reinforcement
Diverse Formats	Content is delivered via text, audio, video, and dialogue
Augments Teachers	Teachers can focus on creative teaching and mentoring
Scalable	Works across different education systems and geographies

In Summary

These real-world examples prove that **GenAI is more than just a futuristic idea**—it's already **empowering students, supporting teachers, and redefining classrooms**. Whether it's in test preparation, foundational subjects, or personalized tutoring, GenAI is enhancing how, when, and what students learn.

TRADITIONAL ASSESSMENTS VS. AI-BASED EVALUATIONS

The way we evaluate student learning is undergoing a major shift. Traditional assessments—think standardized tests, written exams, and paper-based assignments—have long been the standard. But in the age of technology, particularly with the rise of **Generative AI (GenAI)** and intelligent systems, **AI-based evaluations** are offering **more dynamic, continuous, and personalized alternatives**.

Let's compare the two:

Traditional Assessments: The Old School Approach

Key Features:

- Fixed tests at scheduled intervals (e.g., midterms, finals)
- Same questions for all students
- Manual grading by teachers
- Often evaluates memorization more than understanding

Limitations:

- Doesn't adapt to individual learning styles or pace
- Stress-inducing and rigid
- Lacks immediate feedback

- Often biased toward students who perform well under pressure

Example:

A high school math exam with 10 fixed problems administered to the entire class. Everyone gets the same paper, regardless of their current skill level.

AI-Based Evaluations: The Smart Approach

Key Features:

- Continuous assessment based on student interaction
- Adaptive questioning based on performance
- Real-time feedback and suggestions
- Evaluates critical thinking, creativity, and conceptual understanding

Benefits:

- **Personalized Difficulty:** Questions adjust automatically—if a student struggles, the system simplifies; if they excel, it gets harder.
- **Instant Feedback:** Students see what they got wrong and why, immediately.
- **Holistic Evaluation:** AI can assess more than correct answers—like learning behavior, problem-solving steps, and emotional engagement.
- **Time-Efficient for Teachers:** Automates grading and generates insights.

Example:

A GenAI-based platform giving a student math problems that adapt in real-time. If a student takes longer on fractions, the system pauses progression and provides a video tutorial or easier problems for practice.

Side-by-Side Comparison

Feature	Traditional Assessment	AI-Based Evaluation
Frequency	Periodic (e.g., monthly, yearly)	Continuous, real-time
Adaptability	Fixed	Adaptive to learner's pace
Feedback	Delayed	Instant and detailed
Focus	Recall-based	Skill- and understanding-based
Teacher Effort	High (manual grading)	Low (automated)
Personalization	None	Highly personalized
Updates	Infrequent	Continuous learning profile updates

Complementary Roles

Rather than replacing traditional assessments completely, **AI-based evaluations can complement them**. For example:

- Teachers can use **AI insights** to design better exams.
- AI-based formative assessments can guide learners, while summative traditional tests can validate broader learning outcomes.

In Summary

While **traditional assessments** focus on standardization and structure, **AI-based evaluations** emphasize **personalization, continuous improvement, and deeper understanding**. Together, they offer a balanced and modern way to **track student growth and success** in the post-pandemic educational landscape.

CONTINUOUS ASSESSMENT WITH GENAI

In traditional education systems, assessments have often been **episodic**—midterms, finals, or surprise quizzes that happen at fixed intervals. However, in the era of **GenAI-powered learning**, assessment is no longer an event—it becomes a **continuous and integrated process** that happens in the background, in real-time, and in sync with the learner's progress.

What is Continuous Assessment?

Continuous assessment refers to an **ongoing evaluation** of a student's learning journey. It's not about one-time tests but about **tracking growth, identifying gaps, and providing timely interventions** across the learning timeline.

How GenAI Powers Continuous Assessment

GenAI systems—like those embedded in learning platforms or virtual tutors—use **natural language processing (NLP)**, **machine learning**, and **real-time analytics** to evaluate students continuously based on their interactions.

Here's how it works:

1. **Activity Monitoring**
   GenAI observes how students engage with content—what they click, how long they stay, which problems they attempt, how they solve them, and even their emotional cues (if multimodal AI is used).

2. **Adaptive Testing**
   Instead of fixed quizzes, GenAI provides **ongoing micro-assessments**—questions or tasks tailored to current performance and understanding.

3. **Instant Feedback Loops**
   GenAI immediately evaluates the input, provides **corrections, suggestions**, or even explains concepts through conversational AI or multimedia.

4. **Learning Path Optimization**
   Based on these ongoing evaluations, GenAI **adjusts the learning path**, suggests supplementary resources, or slows down/speeds up content delivery.

Benefits of GenAI in Continuous Assessment

Feature	Impact
Personalized Evaluation	Every student is assessed on their own path, strengths, and challenges
Real-Time Insights	Teachers and students receive instant analytics
Frequent Feedback	Encourages reflection and improvement without fear of failure
Early Intervention	Identifies struggling learners early, enabling support before it's too late
Motivation Boost	Celebrates small wins and milestones, keeping learners engaged

Example in Action

Imagine a GenAI tutor helping a student with algebra. As the student solves equations:

- The AI notes if the student repeatedly struggles with factoring.
- It pauses the current path to recommend a visual lesson on factoring.
- After a few interactive examples, it gives a new problem.
- If performance improves, the system progresses; if not, it shifts tactics.

This **loop of assess → adapt → assist → assess again** is the essence of GenAI-powered continuous assessment.

The Role of Teachers

GenAI doesn't replace educators—it **empowers them**:

- Teachers receive **dashboards of student progress**.
- They can spot trends, tailor interventions, and free up time for emotional and creative mentoring.
- Continuous assessment data allows them to **target lesson plans** and support students more effectively.

Considerations

While powerful, continuous assessment through GenAI should also consider:

- **Privacy and consent** in data collection
- **Bias mitigation** in AI decision-making
- **Transparency** in how evaluations influence student records

In Summary

Continuous assessment with GenAI represents a paradigm shift—where learning is no longer judged by isolated scores, but by a **dynamic understanding of growth**. It allows for a **more humane, customized, and insightful** education model that responds to the learner, every step of the way.

REAL-TIME FEEDBACK: HOW GENAI ENHANCES STUDENT PERFORMANCE

In the traditional classroom, students often have to wait hours, days, or even weeks to get feedback on their assignments or tests. By the time they receive it, the moment of learning may have passed. With **Generative AI (GenAI)**, feedback becomes **instantaneous**, **personalized**, and **actionable**—reshaping how students learn and grow.

What is Real-Time Feedback?

Real-time feedback refers to the immediate response a learner receives during or immediately after an activity, enabling quick correction, deeper understanding, and ongoing engagement.

With **GenAI**, this feedback is not only fast—it's smart. It analyzes student inputs in real time, identifies mistakes or gaps, and offers **targeted guidance**, all within the learning experience.

How GenAI Delivers Real-Time Feedback

1. **Natural Language Understanding (NLU):**
   GenAI can interpret written or spoken student responses with human-like understanding.

2. **Immediate Analysis:**

It evaluates the response, identifies errors or misconceptions, and compares it to thousands of similar data points.

3. **Personalized Suggestions:**
Instead of generic corrections, GenAI suggests alternatives, hints, or explanations based on the student's unique learning profile.

4. **Interactive Dialogue:**
Through chatbots or voice assistants, students can ask "why" or "how," prompting the GenAI to elaborate or clarify.

Example Scenario

A student is writing an essay on climate change. As they type:

- GenAI highlights grammar issues, but also suggests more precise vocabulary.

- It identifies weak arguments and suggests how to strengthen them.

- If the student uses a misunderstood concept, GenAI explains it instantly and suggests resources for improvement.

This all happens **as the student writes**, making the learning process **collaborative, not corrective**.

Benefits of Real-Time Feedback

Benefit	Description
Instant Corrections	Mistakes are addressed immediately, preventing the reinforcement of errors.
Deeper Understanding	Learners are encouraged to reflect and revise in the moment.
Targeted Improvement	Feedback is specific to each

	learner's pace, gaps, and strengths.
Motivation Boost	Timely success and correction improve engagement and confidence.
Continuous Growth	Ongoing micro-improvements lead to better long-term outcomes.

The Teacher's Role

Teachers can use GenAI-driven insights to:

- Track how students respond to feedback.
- Identify who needs extra help.
- Customize instruction based on aggregated real-time data.

Far from replacing teachers, GenAI **augments their ability to deliver personalized attention**.

Ethical and Design Considerations

While powerful, real-time feedback systems must ensure:

- **Accuracy:** Misleading feedback can demotivate or confuse learners.
- **Transparency:** Students should understand why certain feedback is given.
- **Tone:** Feedback should be encouraging and constructive, not punitive.

In Summary

Real-time feedback through GenAI transforms the classroom from a place of periodic evaluation to a dynamic space of **constant growth and support**. By giving learners **immediate, intelligent, and tailored responses**, GenAI empowers them to take ownership of their learning and accelerate their academic success.

THE ETHICAL IMPLICATIONS OF AI IN GRADING AND EVALUATION

As AI systems, especially GenAI, become integral to education, one of their most significant applications is **automated grading and evaluation**. While this brings unprecedented speed and scalability, it also raises critical **ethical concerns**. It's essential to examine not only what AI *can* do in grading, but what it *should* do.

What Is AI-Based Grading?

AI-based grading refers to the use of algorithms, often powered by machine learning and natural language processing (NLP), to **assess student work**, especially assignments, essays, and even verbal or coding tasks.

AI systems can:

- Grade multiple-choice or short-answer questions automatically.
- Evaluate written essays for grammar, coherence, and argument quality.
- Assess spoken responses for fluency and accuracy.
- Offer feedback in real-time and provide predictive insights on performance.

Ethical Concerns to Consider

1. Bias in AI Models

AI systems learn from historical data, which may reflect societal biases (e.g., gender, ethnicity, language proficiency). If training data is biased, AI may:

- Undervalue non-native language structures.
- Favor writing styles similar to training sets.
- Penalize creativity or alternative approaches.

Solution: Developers must actively **audit datasets**, use diverse training inputs, and build **bias-mitigation layers**.

2. Lack of Transparency (The Black Box Problem)

AI algorithms, particularly deep learning models, often do not provide clear explanations for their grading decisions.

This raises questions:

- Why did the AI assign this grade?
- On what basis did it deduct marks?

Solution: Promote **explainable AI** that gives feedback not just in scores but in reasoning (e.g., "Your argument lacked evidence").

3. Over-Reliance on Automation

While AI can efficiently grade assignments, **full automation may undermine human judgment** and empathy.

AI may miss:

- Subtle humor, satire, or cultural context.
- Nuanced creative expression.
- Emotional cues or intent behind student work.

Solution: Use AI as a **co-evaluator** or assistant—not a sole authority. Human oversight should always remain.

4. Student Privacy and Data Security

Grading systems rely on **analyzing student data**, which may include:

- Personal information
- Writing styles
- Behavioral patterns

Mismanagement can lead to **data breaches or misuse**.

Solution: Enforce strict **data governance policies**, anonymize data where possible, and comply with regulations like GDPR or FERPA.

5. Fairness and Accessibility

Not all students have equal access to the same digital tools or possess the same digital literacy. An AI that grades code, essays, or presentations might disadvantage:

- Students unfamiliar with digital platforms.
- Those with learning disabilities or ESL backgrounds.

Solution: Design **inclusive AI** systems that adapt to varied learning needs and provide alternatives or support where needed.

The Role of Educators and Policymakers

Teachers, administrators, and policymakers must:

- Establish **clear guidelines** on where and how AI is used.
- Ensure **transparency and consent** from students and parents.
- Monitor AI systems for consistent quality and fairness.

AI should **augment human capabilities**, not replace the thoughtful judgment of educators.

In Summary

AI in grading offers speed, consistency, and scalability—but it must be wielded with caution. Ethical AI in education should be:

- **Fair** – Free of bias
- **Transparent** – Explainable decisions
- **Supportive** – Complementing human evaluators
- **Secure** – Protecting student data
- **Inclusive** – Accessible to all learners

By keeping ethics at the core, we can harness AI's power **without compromising human dignity, creativity, or equity** in education.

THE ROLE OF TEACHERS IN A GENAI-POWERED CLASSROOM

In a world where **Generative AI (GenAI)** can deliver content, assess students, and provide personalized feedback in real time, one might wonder: *What is the role of the teacher?*

The answer is simple yet profound—**more important than ever**.

Rather than being replaced, teachers are being **empowered** by GenAI to focus on what they do best: **mentoring, inspiring, guiding, and supporting** human learners.

Shifting Roles in the Classroom

In a GenAI-powered learning environment, the role of the teacher evolves in the following key ways:

1. Facilitators of Learning, Not Sole Knowledge Providers

- Traditional Role: Delivering lectures and content.
- GenAI-Enhanced Role: Guiding students in navigating AI-generated content, asking critical questions, and encouraging exploration.

Teachers curate resources, personalize learning paths, and help students interpret and synthesize knowledge.

2. Emotional Intelligence & Mentorship

- GenAI cannot replace human empathy.
- Teachers help students manage stress, develop social-emotional skills, and build resilience—essential for holistic development.

They create safe spaces for discussion, debate, and vulnerability.

3. Ethical Guardians and Critical Thinkers

- Teachers help students distinguish between AI-generated content and truth.
- They lead discussions on digital ethics, bias in AI, and responsible use of technology.

By promoting **media literacy and ethical thinking**, teachers shape thoughtful citizens of tomorrow.

4. Designers of Learning Experiences

- Teachers now **collaborate with AI tools** to design interactive simulations, gamified lessons, and personalized projects.
- They orchestrate **blended environments** that integrate GenAI, VR, AR, and collaborative tools to enhance engagement.

5. Interpreters of Data-Driven Insights

GenAI offers real-time dashboards on student performance, learning gaps, and behavioral patterns.

Teachers analyze this data to:

- Identify students at risk.
- Adjust pacing or strategies.
- Offer timely support and interventions.

6. Co-learners and Innovators

As GenAI evolves, teachers become **lifelong learners**, experimenting with new tools and adapting to pedagogical innovation.

They foster a culture of **co-learning**, where students and teachers explore technology together.

Example in Action

A science teacher uses GenAI to:

- Generate personalized assignments based on each student's level.
- Offer real-time feedback during lab simulations.
- Review AI-suggested insights on student progress.

Meanwhile, the teacher focuses on:

- Discussing real-world applications.
- Encouraging group collaboration and inquiry.
- Mentoring students through their learning journey.

Empowering, Not Replacing

Instead of replacing teachers, GenAI **amplifies their superpowers**:

Traditional Teacher	GenAI-Powered Teacher
Delivers lessons	Designs dynamic experiences
Grades assignments	Offers real-time mentorship
Monitors progress	Uses AI dashboards to personalize support
Manages classrooms	Builds human connection and community

In Summary

In GenAI-powered classrooms, **teachers are not obsolete —they're irreplaceable**. Their role shifts from knowledge transmitters to **nurturers of curiosity, creativity, and character**. GenAI becomes their assistant, but the teacher remains the **heart of education**.

Together, human wisdom and artificial intelligence can redefine learning for a brighter, more inclusive future.

COLLABORATIVE TEACHING: TEACHERS AND AI CO-TEACHING

In the age of GenAI, the concept of **"co-teaching"** is no longer limited to two human instructors. Now, it's about the **synergy between teachers and AI** working together to deliver an enriched, responsive, and adaptive learning experience.

Rather than viewing AI as a competitor, it should be seen as a **collaborative partner**—a digital co-teacher that enhances the effectiveness and reach of human educators.

What is Co-Teaching with AI?

Collaborative teaching with GenAI refers to a learning environment where:

- **Teachers and GenAI systems share instructional responsibilities.**
- AI handles routine, repetitive, or data-driven tasks.
- Teachers focus on higher-order skills like empathy, creativity, and critical thinking facilitation.

It's a **partnership**, not a replacement.

Roles of Each Co-Teacher

Human Teacher	GenAI Co-Teacher
Builds relationships,	Delivers personalized content

mentors, and motivates	and feedback
Understands emotional and social contexts	Analyzes patterns in student performance
Guides classroom dynamics	Automates grading, quizzes, and recommendations
Encourages open discussions and critical thinking	Simulates real-world problems or tutoring scenarios

How It Works in Practice

Imagine a classroom where:

- **GenAI generates custom learning materials** based on students' strengths and weaknesses.
- The teacher uses those materials to **guide group discussions** or one-on-one mentoring.
- AI provides **instant quizzes and explanations**, while the teacher steps in for **conceptual clarity or deeper insights**.
- Together, they provide **real-time intervention** and **continuous feedback**.

This is **co-teaching reimagined**.

Benefits of Teacher-AI Collaboration

1. **Time Efficiency**
   - AI takes care of administrative tasks like grading, freeing teachers to focus on teaching.

2. **Hyper-Personalization**
   - Every student receives targeted content without burdening the teacher with extra planning.

3. **Data-Driven Insights**
   - Teachers get real-time analytics on individual and group performance to inform strategy.

4. **Scalability of Quality Education**
   - GenAI helps maintain consistent quality across larger student cohorts.

5. **Balanced Learning**
   - AI supports logic and structure, while teachers nurture emotional intelligence and social skills.

Examples of AI Co-Teaching in Action

- **AI-Tutored Labs**: Students complete AI-guided simulations while the teacher monitors progress and offers additional coaching.

- **Essay Evaluation**: AI provides preliminary grading with feedback; the teacher reviews nuanced aspects like creativity or tone.

- **Group Projects**: AI helps organize and assign tasks; teachers ensure collaboration and evaluate group dynamics.

Challenges to Consider

- **Dependence on Technology**: Over-reliance on AI can reduce human interaction if not managed wisely.

- **Bias in AI Tools**: Teachers must review AI outcomes critically.

- **Teacher Training**: Educators need support to adopt and integrate AI tools effectively.

The Future of Co-Teaching

As GenAI continues to evolve, the teacher's role will grow even more strategic:

- **Orchestrators of learning experiences**
- **Ethical guides in digital environments**
- **Human touch in an AI-enhanced world**

Together, teachers and GenAI can deliver **smarter, fairer, and more inspiring education** for all.

HOW GENAI CAN FREE UP TEACHERS' TIME FOR CREATIVE AND EMOTIONAL ENGAGEMENT

Teaching has never just been about textbooks and tests. The most impactful teachers are those who **inspire creativity**, **connect emotionally**, and **spark curiosity** in their students. However, the reality of modern education often burdens teachers with **administrative work, repetitive tasks, and rigid schedules**, leaving little time for what truly matters.

Enter **Generative AI (GenAI)** — not to replace teachers, but to **liberate them**.

What Drains Teachers' Time?

Teachers are often overwhelmed by:

- Grading repetitive assignments and exams
- Preparing lesson plans for diverse learners
- Answering recurring questions
- Creating quizzes and assessments
- Tracking student progress and behavior
- Reporting and paperwork

These necessary but time-consuming activities often leave **less energy for human-centered teaching**.

How GenAI Reduces the Burden

By automating repetitive tasks and offering intelligent support, GenAI helps teachers reclaim time:

Task	How GenAI Helps
Grading	Auto-evaluates objective and subjective answers with detailed feedback
Lesson Planning	Suggests personalized plans based on class performance and learning goals
Content Creation	Generates slides, quizzes, summaries, and visual aids
Student Queries	Handles basic questions via chatbots or interactive AI assistants
Progress Reports	Analyzes data and creates detailed insights in minutes

The Result: More Time for What Truly Matters

Freed from routine work, teachers can focus on:

1. **Creativity in the Classroom**
   - Designing engaging projects, simulations, and creative exercises
   - Exploring new teaching methods and technologies

2. **Emotional Engagement**
   - Building meaningful relationships with students
   - Supporting mental health, motivation, and emotional growth

3. **One-on-One Mentoring**
   - Offering personalized guidance to students with learning gaps
   - Encouraging gifted learners to push boundaries

4. **Collaborative Learning**
   - Facilitating debates, teamwork, and interactive sessions
   - Creating space for student voices and agency

Example in Action

A literature teacher uses GenAI to:

- Auto-grade essay drafts and suggest edits
- Summarize chapters and extract key literary devices
- Track reading comprehension across the class

With this support, the teacher spends class time:

- Hosting Socratic seminars
- Encouraging students to write their own short stories
- Offering emotional support to a student struggling with confidence

The classroom becomes a **creative and human experience—** powered by AI, but driven by empathy.

Teacher Testimonials

"GenAI took care of 80% of my grading last semester. I used that time to organize a student drama club."
— High School English Teacher

"I finally had time to sit down with each student and talk about their goals. That changed everything."
— Middle School Math Teacher

In Summary

GenAI is not about *replacing* teachers—it's about **redefining their role**. When teachers are freed from monotonous tasks, they become what they were always meant to be: **creative leaders, emotional anchors, and catalysts for lifelong learning**.

By leveraging GenAI, we can create a classroom where **technology supports humanity**, and teachers have the time and space to do what they do best—**inspire**.

EMPOWERING TEACHERS WITH AI-DRIVEN TOOLS AND RESOURCES

As education rapidly evolves in the digital era, **teachers remain the heart of the learning process**. But even the most passionate educators need **support, inspiration, and tools** to manage increasing responsibilities and diverse classrooms. That's where **AI-driven tools** come into play—not as replacements, but as powerful **allies**.

By empowering teachers with intelligent technologies, we enable them to **teach smarter, engage deeper, and lead stronger**.

What Are AI-Driven Tools in Education?

AI-driven tools in the classroom are software platforms or applications that use **artificial intelligence algorithms** to assist teachers in:

- Content creation
- Classroom management
- Student assessment
- Behavior tracking
- Differentiated instruction

- Real-time performance monitoring

These tools **learn and adapt**, helping teachers make **data-informed decisions** without the complexity of manual analysis.

Key Categories of AI-Powered Tools

Category	Examples	Benefits
Lesson Planning	Curipod, Eduaide.AI	Instantly generate customized lesson plans
Content Creation	Canva Magic Write, ChatGPT	Create worksheets, quizzes, slides in minutes
Assessment Tools	Gradescope, Quizizz AI	Automate grading, generate adaptive quizzes
Student Analytics	Classcraft, DreamBox	Identify struggling students early
Virtual Teaching Assistants	Khanmigo, ChatGPT-based bots	Answer FAQs, guide learners after class hours
Professional Development	AI-curated PD platforms	Suggest articles, courses, and communities based on goals

How These Tools Empower Teachers

1. **Time-Saving**
   Routine tasks like quiz creation, grading, and tracking progress are automated—freeing up time for creative instruction.

2. **Informed Instruction**
   AI tools analyze class and individual performance, allowing teachers to tailor their strategies with precision.

3. **Increased Engagement**

Personalized and interactive content keeps students more involved, reducing behavioral issues and improving outcomes.

4. **Professional Growth**
   AI suggests teaching strategies, updates on best practices, and helps teachers grow with ongoing insights.

5. **Inclusivity and Equity**
   Tools can translate languages, adjust reading levels, and adapt content to support all learners, including those with special needs.

Real-World Example

A science teacher uses an AI-powered tool to:

- Generate a personalized lesson plan for each topic
- Assess student understanding using auto-generated quizzes
- Provide differentiated homework based on student ability
- Get weekly AI insights on class performance trends

As a result, the teacher spends less time preparing and more time **engaging students in hands-on experiments, discussions, and mentorship.**

Empowerment in Action

"AI doesn't take my place—it gives me space. I can finally teach the way I always wanted to."
— Primary School Teacher

"With AI handling the admin, I've rediscovered the joy of connecting with my students."
— High School Educator

The Future: Teacher as a Tech-Enabled Leader

In GenAI-enhanced classrooms, the teacher transforms into a:

- **Learning designer**
- **Mentor and motivator**
- **Data-informed strategist**
- **Agent of emotional and creative development**

With AI as a co-pilot, teachers are **not just surviving, but thriving**—redefining education for a dynamic, personalized, and inclusive future.

CLOSING THE ACHIEVEMENT GAP WITH AI

The **achievement gap**—the disparity in academic performance between groups of students, especially those defined by socioeconomic status, race, ethnicity, or disability—has long been a pressing issue in education. Despite policy efforts and educational reforms, **systemic inequalities** have persisted.

However, with the rise of **Artificial Intelligence (AI)**, especially **Generative AI (GenAI)**, we now have **powerful tools to address these disparities** head-on and personalize learning for all students, regardless of their background.

What Causes the Achievement Gap?

- **Unequal access** to quality resources (internet, books, tutors)
- **Language barriers**
- **Learning disabilities or neurodiversity**
- **Teacher shortages or underfunded schools**
- **Limited parental involvement due to work or language challenges**
- **Cultural bias in curriculum or assessments**

AI, when thoughtfully implemented, **targets these root causes** with precision and scalability.

How AI Helps Bridge the Gap

1. Personalized Learning at Scale

AI systems adjust difficulty levels, pacing, and formats based on individual learning needs.

- Struggling students receive more practice and simpler explanations.
- Advanced learners are challenged with deeper content.

Example: An AI tutor identifies that a student has difficulty with fractions and automatically tailors exercises with visual aids and real-world scenarios.

2. Language Support and Real-Time Translation

AI-driven tools can translate classroom instructions, assignments, and lessons in real time.

- Helps English Language Learners (ELLs) keep pace.
- Encourages inclusion and reduces the language barrier.

Example: AI-enabled subtitles allow a Spanish-speaking student to understand an English science video in real time.

3. Early Detection of Learning Gaps

AI analyzes patterns in student performance and flags issues early.

- Teachers get alerts about potential learning delays.
- Timely intervention prevents small gaps from becoming long-term deficits.

Example: A reading platform powered by AI identifies students falling behind in comprehension and suggests targeted reading material.

4. Affordable Access to Quality Education

AI tools are **scalable and low-cost**, providing high-quality education content to underserved regions and communities.

- 24/7 access to AI tutors
- Adaptive platforms available on mobile devices
- Open-source learning resources enhanced by GenAI

Example: A student in a remote village uses an AI-powered app to study algebra without needing a private tutor.

5. Culturally Relevant and Bias-Free Learning

AI, when trained on inclusive data, can help **reduce cultural bias** in content and offer **representation** in learning materials.

- Students see themselves reflected in stories, examples, and characters.
- Encourages motivation and identity development.

Measurable Impact

Studies are beginning to show that:

- AI-powered interventions can raise test scores and engagement levels among disadvantaged learners.
- Educators using AI insights can **reduce dropout rates** and increase college readiness.

AI Supports, But Doesn't Replace, Teachers

It's important to note that **AI doesn't solve the achievement gap alone**—it enables educators to:

- Focus more on relationship-building
- Deliver tailored support
- Make informed, data-backed decisions

In Summary

Closing the achievement gap requires not just compassion and effort—but also smart, equitable tools. With AI:

- Every learner gets a fair shot.
- Learning becomes **adaptive, inclusive, and student-centered**.
- The classroom transforms into a place where **no one is left behind**.

By empowering teachers and personalizing learning, AI can help build a **more just and equal education system**—one student at a time.

MAKING EDUCATION ACCESSIBLE FOR ALL: STUDENTS WITH DISABILITIES

Inclusive education isn't just a philosophy—it's a **commitment to equity**, ensuring every learner, regardless of their physical, cognitive, or sensory abilities, receives a quality education. With the advent of **Artificial Intelligence (AI)** and **Generative AI (GenAI)**, we now have the tools to **break down longstanding barriers** and **make education truly accessible** for students with disabilities.

The Accessibility Challenge

Students with disabilities often face multiple obstacles in traditional classrooms:

- Inaccessible teaching materials
- Limited physical access to facilities
- Inadequate teacher training
- One-size-fits-all assessment methods
- Social stigma and isolation

Despite progress through assistive technologies, many gaps remain. GenAI offers **new levels of adaptability, personalization, and autonomy**.

How GenAI and AI Transform Accessibility

1. Text-to-Speech and Speech-to-Text Capabilities

AI converts written text into spoken words and vice versa—essential for:

- Students with visual impairments
- Learners with dyslexia
- Those with motor challenges

Example: A student with limited motor function dictates an essay to an AI-powered writing assistant.

2. Real-Time Captioning and Translation

GenAI can provide instant captions and language translations for audio/video content.

- Helps students with hearing impairments
- Assists students who use sign language
- Supports multilingual learners

Example: A hearing-impaired student watches a live-streamed science class with real-time AI-generated captions.

3. Personalized Learning Interfaces

AI-powered platforms adapt not only the content but also the **mode of delivery**:

- Large fonts and high-contrast visuals for the visually impaired
- Simplified content with icons for students with cognitive disabilities
- Switch-accessible navigation for those with motor impairments

Example: A student with autism uses an AI-based system that delivers instructions visually, with calming color schemes and predictable routines.

4. Emotion Recognition and Behavioral Support

Advanced AI can analyze facial expressions, tone of voice, and behavior to detect distress, confusion, or disengagement.

- Enables timely intervention
- Supports social-emotional learning for neurodiverse students

Example: A GenAI assistant recognizes that a student is struggling emotionally and notifies the teacher to provide one-on-one support.

5. Smart Assistive Devices

From AI-powered wheelchairs to voice-activated whiteboards, AI-integrated tools **increase independence**.

- Helps students control devices via voice or eye-tracking
- Promotes inclusion in all learning environments

Empowering Educators and Institutions

AI tools also support teachers by:

- Offering **IEP (Individualized Education Program) recommendations**
- Suggesting **adaptive strategies**
- Monitoring **student progress** and alerting for early interventions

Educators are no longer alone in accommodating diverse needs—AI acts as a **real-time partner** in creating inclusive classrooms.

A Future Where No One is Left Behind

By combining **compassionate teaching** with **AI-driven**

personalization, we can ensure:

- Every student is seen, heard, and supported
- Disability does not equate to disadvantage
- Education becomes a level playing field for all

Final Thought

"Accessibility is not about helping a few—it's about designing for everyone."

With AI and GenAI, we can **reimagine education** as a system that works **for every mind, every body, and every learner.**

BREAKING GEOGRAPHICAL BARRIERS: EDUCATION FOR REMOTE AND RURAL AREAS

Access to quality education has traditionally been **uneven**, especially in **remote and rural regions**. Factors such as poor infrastructure, lack of qualified teachers, limited resources, and social inequality have long hindered educational development in these areas. But today, with the advancement of **AI and GenAI technologies**, we are witnessing a powerful shift—where **education can reach every corner of the world**, regardless of geography.

The Rural Education Challenge

Students in rural or isolated regions often face:

- Shortage of subject-specialist teachers
- Long travel distances to schools
- Outdated textbooks or lack of digital tools
- Limited exposure to global knowledge

- Language and cultural isolation

These issues contribute to **lower literacy rates, high dropout rates**, and **less access to higher education** opportunities.

How GenAI Bridges the Distance

1. Virtual Classrooms and AI Tutors

AI-powered learning platforms enable students to:

- Attend virtual classes in real-time or on-demand
- Interact with AI tutors that provide 24/7 assistance
- Learn at their own pace and convenience

Example: A student in a Himalayan village logs into a GenAI platform that teaches biology through voice, video, and adaptive Q&A—even without a subject teacher nearby.

2. Low-Bandwidth Adaptive Solutions

GenAI tools are becoming increasingly optimized for:

- **Offline access** with downloadable modules
- Operation on **low-cost smartphones and tablets**
- Smart compression for **rural connectivity**

Example: An AI-enabled mobile app downloads daily lessons during weak signal hours and allows a child in a tribal village to study offline during the day.

3. Multilingual and Localized Content

GenAI can:

- Translate learning content into local dialects
- Generate culturally relevant examples and stories
- Bridge language gaps that often alienate rural learners

Example: A GenAI tool explains mathematics in Bhojpuri for students in Bihar, using local currency and market examples for relatability.

4. Remote Teacher Training and Support

Educators in rural areas benefit from AI-powered:

- Virtual mentoring and upskilling
- Automated lesson planning and content suggestions
- Real-time feedback on teaching effectiveness

Example: A teacher in a tribal school receives AI-generated guidance on inclusive pedagogy and curriculum alignment.

5. Community-Based Learning Networks

With GenAI, entire communities can be involved:

- Parent-facing AI assistants guide home learning
- Local youth are trained to become tech facilitators
- Mobile learning vans and solar-powered classrooms extend access

Example: A solar-powered GenAI-enabled classroom-on-wheels brings education to children in remote parts of Rajasthan every week.

Long-Term Impact

- **Improved enrollment and retention** in rural schools
- **Equal opportunities** for competitive exams and career pathways
- Empowerment of girls and marginalized communities
- **Decentralization of knowledge** from urban hubs to every village

A Global Vision

"Where you live should never determine what you learn."

With GenAI, we are moving closer to **education without borders** —where children from rural plains to forested hills can **learn, dream, and achieve** on equal footing with urban peers.

HOW GENAI CAN HELP IN DEVELOPING COUNTRIES EDUCATION SYSTEMS

Education in developing countries often grapples with **limited infrastructure, teacher shortages, unequal access**, and outdated materials. But the rise of **Generative AI (GenAI)** offers a transformative opportunity to **leapfrog traditional barriers** and build smarter, more inclusive, and scalable educational systems.

The Educational Hurdles in Developing Nations

Many developing countries face:

- A lack of **trained teachers**, especially in STEM subjects.
- Overcrowded classrooms and **low teacher-student ratios**.
- **Inadequate learning materials** and technology.
- **Language barriers** in multilingual populations.
- **Urban-rural educational divides**.
- High dropout rates and **gender disparities** in schooling.

These challenges hinder **quality learning outcomes**, limit career opportunities, and slow economic development.

GenAI: A Catalyst for Educational Transformation

GenAI brings a powerful toolkit to reshape the education landscape:

1. Automated and Scalable Content Creation

GenAI can:

- Generate **syllabus-aligned lesson plans** in minutes.
- Translate content into **multiple local languages**.
- Provide **interactive quizzes, summaries, and visual aids**.

Example: A rural school in Ghana uses GenAI to generate daily science lessons in both English and Twi, supporting bilingual education with minimal manual effort.

2. Virtual Teaching Assistants

Where teacher shortages exist, GenAI acts as:

- A **24/7 tutor** answering student questions.
- An assistant that **explains complex topics** step-by-step.
- A mentor that adjusts instruction based on the learner's pace.

Example: Students in a slum area of Nairobi access a chatbot on shared tablets to revise math topics after school hours, guided in their native language.

3. Low-Cost, Offline-Friendly Learning Tools

GenAI can be embedded into:

- Mobile apps that **work offline** with periodic syncs.
- **SMS- or voice-based learning systems** for non-smartphone users.

- Devices that require **minimal data and electricity**.

Example: A solar-powered classroom in a remote village of Nepal runs a GenAI system that stores educational materials locally and updates weekly through low-bandwidth connections.

4. Personalized and Inclusive Education

GenAI enables:

- **Adaptive learning paths** for different learning speeds.
- **Customized resources** for students with disabilities.
- Culturally appropriate content that resonates with diverse backgrounds.

Example: In Bangladesh, a GenAI tool personalizes reading material for students with visual impairments using text-to-speech and Braille-support tools.

5. Training and Empowering Teachers

GenAI helps teachers by:

- Recommending **instructional strategies**.
- Providing **real-time feedback** on classroom performance.
- Offering **micro-learning modules** for ongoing development.

Example: Teachers in rural India use a GenAI coach that provides lesson suggestions aligned with the national curriculum and local contexts.

6. Policy-Making and Data-Driven Decisions

Governments can use AI tools for:

- Tracking **student performance** and dropout trends.
- Planning **resource allocation** more effectively.

- Designing **evidence-based education reforms**.

Example: The Ministry of Education in Kenya uses AI analytics to identify districts with the highest gender disparity in school attendance and allocate support accordingly.

Long-Term Impact of GenAI in Developing Nations

- **Bridges the rural-urban education gap**
- Reduces **gender and language-based inequalities**
- Cultivates **future-ready skills** like digital literacy and problem-solving
- Promotes **economic upliftment** through education

Final Thought

"GenAI doesn't just digitize education—it democratizes it."

For developing countries, GenAI presents an opportunity to **build stronger, fairer, and more resilient education systems**, even in the face of limited resources.

TECHNOLOGICAL BARRIERS: INFRASTRUCTURE AND ACCESS

While GenAI has the potential to revolutionize education across the globe, its success greatly depends on the **technological infrastructure** available to support it. In many parts of the world —especially in developing regions—**technological barriers** such as poor connectivity, lack of devices, and inadequate digital literacy can hinder the equitable implementation of GenAI-powered education.

1. Limited Internet Connectivity

Many rural and underserved areas still struggle with:

- **Low bandwidth or no internet access**
- **Unstable or expensive network services**
- Reliance on **2G/3G networks** that can't support AI platforms

Impact: Students can't access GenAI tools like interactive chatbots, real-time feedback systems, or cloud-based learning platforms, which depend heavily on internet availability.

2. Lack of Digital Devices

Students and schools in low-resource areas may lack:

- **Computers or laptops**
- **Smartphones or tablets**
- Smartboards, projectors, or **charging facilities**

Impact: Without access to the hardware needed to interact with GenAI, the digital divide widens, creating inequality in learning opportunities.

3. Inadequate Power Supply

In many developing countries, especially in remote regions:

- **Power outages** are frequent and unpredictable
- Some villages still have **no electricity**
- Charging devices or running a digital classroom becomes a major challenge

Impact: AI tools can't function properly, and even simple digital teaching becomes difficult, leading to interrupted learning.

4. Low Digital Literacy

Teachers, students, and even parents may not:

- Be comfortable using **digital platforms**
- Understand how to operate GenAI interfaces
- Know how to manage online learning environments

Impact: A lack of basic training leads to poor adoption of AI tools, reducing their effectiveness or even making them irrelevant in some cases.

5. Cost and Affordability

While technology is becoming more affordable, many GenAI systems still require:

- **Subscription fees**
- Regular **software updates**

- Investment in **tech maintenance and training**

Impact: Schools with limited budgets may not be able to implement or sustain AI-powered education in the long run.

6. Language and Cultural Barriers

GenAI platforms are often designed with:

- **Western-centric data sets**
- Limited support for **local languages and dialects**
- Content that might not align with cultural values

Impact: Learners may find the material unfamiliar, irrelevant, or difficult to understand, reducing engagement and learning outcomes.

Solutions to Overcome Technological Barriers

1. **Offline and Lightweight AI Models** – Develop GenAI tools that work without continuous internet.
2. **Community Tech Hubs** – Shared devices and internet in community centers or schools.
3. **Government and NGO Support** – Subsidized devices, internet, and training programs.
4. **Teacher Training Programs** – Focused on digital literacy and AI integration.
5. **Solar Power Solutions** – For electricity in off-grid locations.
6. **Localization of AI Tools** – Multilingual, culturally relevant GenAI systems.

Final Thought

"Innovation in education must be matched by innovation in accessibility."

While GenAI holds immense promise, **ensuring inclusive**

access must be a top priority. By addressing these technological barriers head-on, we can work towards a future where **every learner benefits**, regardless of their zip code.

DATA PRIVACY AND SECURITY CONCERNS IN AI-DRIVEN EDUCATION

As educational systems increasingly adopt GenAI and digital platforms, **student data becomes the cornerstone** of personalized learning, performance analysis, and content generation. However, this reliance on data brings with it significant concerns around **privacy, security, and ethical use**.

What Kind of Data is Collected?

AI-driven educational platforms often collect:

- Personal details (name, age, gender, location)
- Academic records and performance
- Behavioral data (how students interact with content)
- Emotional and cognitive feedback (from chatbots or assessments)
- Biometric data (in advanced systems)

Concern: The more data collected, the greater the risk of misuse or breach.

Major Privacy and Security Risks

1. Unauthorized Data Access

Hackers or untrustworthy insiders can gain access to sensitive student and teacher data, leading to identity theft, manipulation, or exploitation.

2. Lack of Informed Consent

Often, students (especially minors) and parents are **unaware** of how their data is being collected, stored, or used by AI systems.

3. Data Misuse by Third Parties

EdTech platforms may **sell or share data** with advertisers, analytics firms, or other organizations without proper disclosure.

4. Algorithmic Bias and Discrimination

Poorly designed AI systems may use biased data, resulting in **unfair grading**, stereotyping, or exclusion of certain student groups.

5. Lack of Clear Regulations

Many countries lack strict **data protection laws** for AI in education, making enforcement difficult and leaving users vulnerable.

Strategies for Mitigating Risks

1. Robust Data Encryption

All student data—both in transit and at rest—should be encrypted to prevent unauthorized access.

2. Role-Based Access Control

Only authorized personnel (e.g., teachers, admin) should access specific data. Limit exposure to what's necessary.

3. Transparent Data Policies

Schools and platforms must clearly explain:

- What data is collected
- Why it's collected

- How it will be used
- Who will have access

4. Regular Security Audits

Educational institutions and AI vendors must conduct **frequent audits** to identify and patch vulnerabilities.

5. User Consent and Control

Students and parents should be empowered to:

- Opt in or out of data collection
- View or delete their data
- Control how their data is used

Legal Frameworks and Best Practices

- **GDPR (EU):** Requires explicit consent, right to be forgotten, and data minimization.
- **FERPA (USA):** Protects the privacy of student education records.
- **India's DPDP Act 2023:** Focuses on digital data protection and consent-driven data use.

Educational platforms must align with these and other regional privacy laws to ensure compliance.

Ethical Considerations

- AI should **respect student autonomy** and human dignity.
- Systems must avoid **profiling or ranking students** in ways that could harm confidence or create pressure.
- Stakeholders should consider **moral responsibility** in deploying AI in sensitive environments like classrooms.

Final Thought

"Protecting student data isn't just a legal obligation—it's a moral one."

As we harness GenAI to reshape education, **trust must be at the core** of every digital interaction. By ensuring robust privacy and security protocols, we can create an AI-powered educational system that is **both innovative and ethical**.

RESISTANCE TO CHANGE: EDUCATORS' RELUCTANCE TO ADOPT AI

Despite the immense potential of GenAI and other digital tools in revolutionizing education, many educators exhibit **resistance or hesitation** toward adopting these technologies. This reluctance stems from a mix of practical, emotional, and philosophical concerns.

---

1. Fear of Job Replacement

One of the most common fears among educators is that **AI may replace teachers** entirely:

- AI systems that automate grading, content delivery, or tutoring can appear to **threaten the traditional teacher role**.
- This leads to anxiety and resistance, especially in communities with **limited tech literacy or job security**.

Reality Check: AI is best viewed as an assistant—not a replacement—meant to **enhance teaching**, not eliminate it.

---

2. Lack of Digital Literacy

Many educators, particularly those with decades of classroom experience, are:

- **Unfamiliar with AI platforms**
- Intimidated by the **complexity of digital tools**
- Concerned about being unable to keep up with evolving technology

Impact: This skill gap makes them less confident and more resistant to integrating AI into their teaching.

3. Unclear Benefits or Outcomes

Some teachers struggle to see the **practical benefits** of using GenAI tools:

- They may question whether AI truly improves learning outcomes.
- Past experiences with **ineffective edtech tools** contribute to skepticism.

Result: Without clear success stories or measurable improvements, there's **little motivation** to change existing methods.

4. Increased Workload During Transition

Introducing GenAI into classrooms requires:

- Time-consuming **training sessions**
- New lesson planning around AI tools
- Trial and error before systems become effective

Short-Term Pain: Many teachers feel overwhelmed and worry that the **initial burden** outweighs the long-term gain.

5. Concerns About Student Engagement

Educators often worry that:

- **Over-reliance on AI** will reduce face-to-face interaction.
- Students may become **passive recipients** of AI-generated content instead of active learners.
- AI may not understand the **emotional nuances** that teachers pick up intuitively.

Belief: True learning involves a human connection that **algorithms can't replicate**.

---

6. Preserving Pedagogical Autonomy

Teachers value the freedom to:

- Choose their teaching methods
- Design custom lesson plans
- Adapt based on real-time classroom dynamics

Fear: AI may impose **standardized models** or limit the **creative freedom** teachers currently enjoy.

Addressing the Resistance: Moving Toward Adoption

1. **Professional Development**
   - Hands-on training, not just theoretical sessions
   - Ongoing mentorship and support

2. **Involve Teachers in Tech Design**
   - Co-create tools with teachers
   - Encourage feedback during pilot phases

3. **Start Small, Scale Gradually**
   - Begin with simple AI features (e.g., automated quizzes)
   - Allow teachers to see results firsthand

4. **Celebrate Educator Success Stories**
   - Highlight teachers who've successfully

integrated AI

- Share measurable student improvements

5. **Ensure AI as a Supportive Tool**
    - Reinforce the message: *"AI augments, not replaces."*

Final Thought

"If we want AI in the classroom, we must first win the hearts of those who lead it."

Educators are the **cornerstone of the learning experience**, and their buy-in is essential. With the right support, training, and reassurance, even the most reluctant teachers can become **AI champions**, reshaping education for generations to come.

ADDRESSING BIAS IN AI ALGORITHMS IN EDUCATION

As AI and GenAI become integral to education—powering content creation, assessment, and personalized learning—it's crucial to recognize that **AI systems can inherit biases** from the data they are trained on. If left unchecked, these biases can perpetuate inequality and lead to unfair treatment of students.

What is Algorithmic Bias?

Algorithmic bias refers to systematic errors in AI systems that result in unfair outcomes, often favoring one group over another based on race, gender, socio-economic status, language, or region.

For example:

- An AI grading system may **consistently give lower scores to students who write in non-native English**, not because their ideas are poor, but because of grammatical patterns it was not trained to understand.
- Recommendation engines might push **more advanced content to boys than girls** due to historical data patterns in STEM subjects.

How Bias Manifests in Educational AI

1. **Biased Training Data**
   - AI models trained on historical data reflecting **existing societal or classroom inequalities** may reinforce those patterns.

2. **Lack of Representation**
   - Students from rural areas, minority communities, or with disabilities might be **underrepresented in training datasets**, leading to poor AI performance for these groups.

3. **Cultural & Linguistic Bias**
   - AI tools may struggle to recognize **diverse expressions or accents**, disadvantaging non-mainstream language users.

4. **Unequal Access to AI Tools**
   - Bias can emerge simply because students **without internet access** or devices are excluded from AI-enhanced learning opportunities.

Why It's Dangerous in Education

- **Reinforces existing inequalities**
- **Erodes student trust in educational systems**
- **Reduces opportunities for underprivileged learners**
- **Limits the fairness and inclusiveness** that education should promote

Strategies to Mitigate Bias

1. Diverse and Inclusive Training Data

- AI models should be trained on **diverse datasets** that represent all student demographics, languages, and learning styles.

- Regular audits of datasets help uncover and correct imbalances.

2. Bias Testing and Auditing

- Institutions must perform **regular bias evaluations** on AI systems.
- Simulated scenarios can help detect if certain student groups are consistently disadvantaged.

3. Human Oversight

- Teachers and educators must remain in the loop to **interpret AI recommendations** and intervene when necessary.
- Final decisions, especially in grading or student assessments, should **never be made by AI alone**.

4. Transparent Algorithms

- Institutions should use **explainable AI (XAI)—** systems that provide clear, understandable reasons behind AI decisions.
- This increases trust and allows stakeholders to identify bias more easily.

5. AI Ethics Guidelines in Education

- Educational boards and governments should establish **ethical frameworks** that guide the development and use of AI tools in learning environments.
- Guidelines should address fairness, accountability, inclusivity, and transparency.

Real-World Initiatives

- **IBM's AI Fairness 360 Toolkit**: Offers open-source tools to detect and mitigate bias in machine learning models.
- **Partnership on AI**: Promotes inclusive AI systems

through cross-sector collaboration.

- **EdTech companies** are increasingly including **bias-detection protocols** in their product development lifecycles.

Final Thought

"In the classroom of the future, fairness should never be optional."

As AI continues to shape how students learn, interact, and get assessed, addressing bias is not just a technical challenge—it's a **moral responsibility**. By ensuring fairness in AI algorithms, we can build an education system that truly serves **every student**, regardless of their background.

THE COST FACTOR: GENAI INTEGRATION IN UNDERFUNDED SCHOOLS

While GenAI promises to revolutionize education with personalized learning, smart assessments, and interactive tools, its **implementation cost** remains a major hurdle—especially for underfunded schools. These institutions often struggle with basic infrastructure, let alone the resources required to integrate advanced technologies.

Understanding the Financial Barriers

1. Lack of Basic Infrastructure

Underfunded schools frequently lack:

- Stable electricity
- High-speed internet
- Modern computer labs
- Adequate devices for students and teachers

Without these essentials, **GenAI integration is almost impossible**, regardless of the tool's potential.

2. High Initial Investment

Deploying GenAI systems involves upfront costs such as:

- Hardware (laptops, tablets, servers)
- Software licenses or subscriptions
- Teacher training programs
- Maintenance and support

These costs can quickly exceed the **limited budgets** of public or rural schools.

3. Recurring Costs

Even if initial funding is managed, ongoing expenses like:

- Internet bandwidth
- Cloud computing services
- Data storage and security
- Software updates

...can be **unsustainable in the long run** without external support.

Teacher Training: A Hidden Cost

GenAI tools are only effective when educators:

- Know how to use them
- Trust the technology
- Integrate them into daily instruction

Training programs are **often expensive and time-consuming**, making them an additional burden for resource-limited schools.

The Equity Dilemma

"Technology should level the playing field, not widen the gap."

When GenAI is only accessible to well-funded schools, it risks creating a **digital divide**:

- Privileged students get hyper-personalized, AI-enhanced education.

- Disadvantaged students fall further behind in outdated classrooms.

This **threatens the core value of equitable education**.

Strategies to Overcome Cost Challenges

1. Open-Source and Low-Cost GenAI Tools

Promote use of open educational resources (OER) and **free or freemium AI tools** tailored for education.

2. Public-Private Partnerships

Tech companies, NGOs, and government bodies can collaborate to:

- Donate devices
- Offer subsidized AI platforms
- Provide teacher training as CSR initiatives

3. Government Grants and Funding Models

Policy frameworks should include **special GenAI funding** for marginalized schools through innovation grants or targeted digital learning budgets.

4. Community-Based Innovation Hubs

Setting up **shared learning labs** in rural areas can pool resources and offer GenAI access to multiple schools.

5. Edge AI and Offline Capabilities

Developing AI tools that **work offline or with minimal internet** can drastically reduce infrastructure dependence.

Conclusion

GenAI holds tremendous potential to uplift education, but its success hinges on **inclusivity and affordability**. Without mindful planning and innovative funding strategies, it may remain a privilege for the few—rather than a transformation for all.

"The future of education must be smart—but also fair."

EMERGING TRENDS AND INNOVATIONS IN GENAI FOR CLASSROOMS

As the post-pandemic educational landscape evolves, **Generative AI (GenAI)** is reshaping classrooms with remarkable speed and creativity. What started as intelligent automation is now expanding into **immersive, personalized, and highly interactive learning ecosystems**. Let's explore the most exciting and impactful trends in GenAI for education.

---

1. AI-Powered Tutoring Assistants

GenAI-powered bots are becoming **on-demand virtual tutors** for students. These assistants:

- Answer subject-specific questions in real time
- Explain complex concepts in personalized ways
- Provide 24/7 homework support

Example: Tools like ChatGPT, Khanmigo, or Google's Gemini are being adapted to serve as digital teaching companions.

---

2. Automated Content Creation

Teachers are using GenAI to:

- Generate quizzes, assignments, and flashcards

- Create lesson plans tailored to individual or class needs
- Develop multiple versions of learning materials to suit diverse learning styles

Example: AI tools like Quizizz, MagicSchool.ai, and Diffit make it easy for teachers to save time while increasing lesson quality.

3. Multilingual and Multimodal Learning

GenAI supports translation, voice synthesis, and visual learning aids, which:

- Help **non-native speakers** access content
- Support **students with disabilities**
- Offer **visual and auditory learning** alternatives

Example: GenAI can translate a history lesson into local languages and even add audio narration or generate comic strips for better understanding.

4. Hyper-Personalized Learning Pathways

GenAI analyzes:

- A student's performance
- Learning pace
- Interests and behavior patterns

...and creates a **custom curriculum**, adapting in real-time as the student progresses.

Example: Adaptive platforms like Squirrel AI or Century Tech adjust content difficulty and format to suit each learner's needs.

5. AI-Generated Simulations and Virtual Labs

Students can now **experiment virtually** in science labs or explore historical events via simulations generated by GenAI.

Example: A biology class could explore a cell in 3D, while a history class could walk through ancient Rome—all powered by generative tools.

6. Emotional AI & Student Sentiment Analysis

GenAI is beginning to detect **student stress, confusion, or disengagement** through facial cues, writing tone, or voice patterns—and can respond accordingly.

Example: An emotionally aware AI might slow down a lesson or switch formats if it detects a student is overwhelmed.

7. Gamified Learning Experiences

GenAI is being used to **design educational games**, quizzes, and story-based learning paths that make studying more fun and addictive.

Example: AI-generated role-play scenarios can turn a history lesson into an adventure game or a math lesson into a treasure hunt.

8. Teacher Copilots and Workflow Automation

Teachers are leveraging AI for:

- Grading essays with feedback
- Creating differentiated instruction plans
- Managing classroom workflows like attendance or progress tracking

Example: Platforms like Copilot for Education or Curipod streamline tasks so teachers can focus more on mentorship.

9. Inclusive and Assistive Learning Tools

GenAI tools are helping students with:

- Dyslexia (text-to-speech)
- Autism (social skill development)
- Visual impairments (image-to-text, audio

descriptions)

These innovations promote **inclusive classrooms** where every learner thrives.

---

10. Secure and Ethical AI in Education

As GenAI usage grows, there's a rising trend in developing:

- **Explainable AI (XAI)** for transparency
- **Privacy-preserving tools** to protect student data
- **Bias-checking mechanisms** to ensure fairness

These innovations ensure GenAI remains **ethical, inclusive, and safe** in educational settings.

The Future Is Now

"GenAI is not just supporting education—it's reinventing it."

The integration of GenAI into classrooms isn't a futuristic dream. It's already unfolding in real-time, making education more engaging, adaptive, and accessible. The key lies in **responsible innovation**, ensuring that every student and teacher benefits from these emerging tools.

THE POTENTIAL OF GENAI IN LIFELONG LEARNING AND ADULT EDUCATION

In today's fast-evolving world, **education doesn't end at graduation.** As industries change and new skills emerge, adults are returning to learning—either to upskill, reskill, or explore personal interests. **Generative AI (GenAI)** is proving to be a powerful enabler of **lifelong learning**, removing traditional barriers and making education more personalized, accessible, and engaging for adults.

Why Lifelong Learning Matters Now More Than Ever

- **Job market volatility** due to automation, AI, and digitization
- Rise of **gig economy** and freelance careers
- Need for **continuous personal growth and adaptability**
- Rapid innovation in sectors like healthcare, fintech, education, and design

Lifelong learning has become a **necessity**, not a luxury.

How GenAI is Transforming Adult Education

1. Personalized Learning Journeys

GenAI tailors content based on:

- Learning goals
- Career background
- Pace of progress
- Preferred learning style

Example: An adult learner aiming to become a data analyst can follow a custom course combining Python, Excel, and machine learning, curated in real-time by GenAI.

2. Microlearning and On-Demand Education

Busy adults prefer **bite-sized learning** that fits into their schedules.

GenAI can generate:

- Short explainer videos
- 10-minute topic summaries
- Daily quiz prompts
- Career-aligned learning paths

Example: A working mother can ask an AI tutor for a 5-minute summary on "Agile project management" while commuting.

3. Language Learning and Communication Skills

GenAI enables adults to:

- Practice foreign languages in real conversations
- Improve writing and grammar
- Simulate business communications (e.g., emails, interviews)

Example: A learner can practice English with an AI-powered virtual tutor who provides corrections and cultural context in real time.

4. Career Coaching and Interview Practice

GenAI tools can simulate:

- Mock interviews
- Resume enhancement
- Role-specific skill assessments
- Portfolio building for creative professionals

Example: A mid-career engineer looking to transition into product management can practice case interviews with a GenAI assistant.

5. Inclusive Education for Diverse Needs

GenAI supports adult learners who may:

- Have disabilities
- Face language barriers
- Lack formal educational backgrounds

Example: Text-to-speech, speech-to-text, and translated lessons help learners with visual impairments or low literacy levels.

6. Affordable Upskilling at Scale

Traditional adult learning can be costly and inaccessible. GenAI makes quality education available at low or no cost.

Example: Instead of enrolling in expensive bootcamps, learners can access AI-generated curriculums, exercises, and feedback through platforms like Coursera, ChatGPT, or Skillsoft AI.

7. AI-Supported Group Learning

GenAI can:

- Moderate peer discussions
- Suggest collaborative projects
- Provide feedback in real-time

This helps adults feel part of a **community**, even in online or asynchronous environments.

Global Impact Potential

- **Rural professionals** can learn global skills with just a phone and internet.
- **Retired individuals** can pursue interests like digital art, writing, or entrepreneurship.
- **Blue-collar workers** can upskill in areas like digital marketing, e-commerce, or logistics management.

Challenges to Address

- **Digital literacy gaps** in older learners
- **Access to technology** and connectivity
- **Data privacy** and trust in AI systems
- **Motivation and retention** over time

Solutions must include user-friendly interfaces, guided pathways, and human-AI hybrid support models.

The Future of Adult Education Is AI-Augmented

"With GenAI, adult learning becomes lifelong, life-wide, and life-deep."

It's not just about getting a certificate—it's about staying relevant, growing as a person, and seizing new opportunities throughout life. GenAI has the potential to **democratize education beyond school walls**, opening doors for millions of learners globally.

WHAT ROLE WILL GENAI PLAY IN UNIVERSITIES AND HIGHER EDUCATION?

Generative AI (GenAI) is poised to **redefine the landscape of universities and higher education**, just as it is transforming primary and secondary education. From research to teaching, administration to student support—GenAI is becoming an integral force in **making higher education smarter, faster, more inclusive, and deeply personalized.**

---

1. Enhancing Research and Innovation

In universities, **research is the heart of advancement**. GenAI can:

- **Analyze large data sets** quickly for trends and correlations
- Generate **literature reviews** and summaries from vast academic databases
- Suggest **hypotheses and models** based on existing knowledge
- Assist in **coding, simulations, and prototyping**

Example: A PhD student in molecular biology can use GenAI to analyze genome sequences and generate experimental pathways.

2. Personalized Learning and Mentorship

GenAI empowers universities to provide:

- Tailored course recommendations
- Real-time learning analytics
- Adaptive learning paths based on student performance and interests
- Virtual mentors for assignments, project guidance, and career planning

Example: A university student struggling with calculus receives AI-generated explanations, exercises, and revision plans that match their learning style.

3. Redefining the Role of Professors

Professors won't be replaced—but **augmented**. GenAI helps educators:

- Automate grading and feedback
- Create personalized content (e.g., quizzes, presentations, case studies)
- Simulate complex phenomena or debates
- Monitor class engagement and tailor instruction

Example: A law professor uses GenAI to generate moot court cases and simulate trial scenarios for students.

4. Global Classrooms and Multilingual Access

GenAI enables:

- **Real-time translation** of lectures and study material
- **Cross-border collaboration** between students and institutions
- Multilingual chatbots for **student support and**

engagement

Example: An engineering course taught in English can be instantly translated for students in Spain, India, or Brazil—enhancing inclusivity.

5. Streamlining University Administration

GenAI is also streamlining behind-the-scenes operations:

- Handling admissions queries through chatbots
- Predicting enrollment trends
- Generating timetables, exam schedules, and performance analytics
- Automating administrative workflows and emails

Example: An AI assistant responds to student emails, updates course registration statuses, and even sends reminders for fee payments.

6. Improving Retention and Student Success

By analyzing behavioral and performance data, GenAI can:

- Detect early signs of disengagement or academic risk
- Recommend intervention strategies
- Provide 24/7 support and guidance
- Enable mental health chatbots and wellbeing monitoring

Example: A student who misses classes and submits late assignments receives nudges, counseling resources, and academic support—all AI-enabled.

7. Supporting Lifelong Learning and Micro-Credentials

Universities are increasingly offering **modular, bite-sized learning** experiences. GenAI can:

- Curate micro-courses on emerging skills

- Help learners navigate certification paths aligned with job markets
- Suggest combinations of courses based on industry trends

Example: A working professional takes a 3-week AI ethics module curated by GenAI, earning a digital badge for LinkedIn.

8. Fostering Critical Thinking and Ethics

While GenAI provides vast knowledge, **students must still be taught to think, question, and evaluate**.

Universities play a key role in:

- Educating students on **AI ethics and responsible use**
- Designing assignments that go **beyond AI-generated answers**
- Encouraging **AI-human collaboration** rather than AI-dependence

Quote: "The goal is not to stop students from using GenAI, but to teach them how to use it wisely."

Challenges Ahead

- Academic integrity: detecting AI-assisted plagiarism
- Skill gaps in faculty for AI usage
- Infrastructure and investment barriers
- Data privacy and transparency in AI usage

Solutions will require **policy frameworks**, **digital training**, and **human-centered AI governance**.

The Future University: Human + AI Partnership

GenAI is not replacing universities—it's **redefining their purpose**: from content delivery to experience creation, from testing memory to cultivating wisdom.

The future of higher education is collaborative, inclusive, lifelong—and powered by GenAI.

THE EVOLUTION OF HUMAN-AI COLLABORATION IN EDUCATION

The journey of artificial intelligence in education has not been one of replacement—but of **collaboration**. From early automation tools to advanced GenAI systems, the synergy between humans and machines in educational settings has evolved significantly, creating richer learning environments and smarter teaching ecosystems.

---

1. The Early Days: Automation and Efficiency

In the beginning, AI's presence in education was largely about **automation**:

- **Computer-Assisted Instruction (CAI)** in the 1960s and 70s enabled basic quizzes and tutorials.
- Learning Management Systems (LMS) introduced in the 1990s helped in scheduling, attendance, and assignment tracking.
- Simple rule-based systems graded multiple-choice questions and offered standardized test prep.

AI was a **tool**, and teachers maintained full control over content, delivery, and interaction.

---

2. Intelligent Tutoring Systems (ITS)

By the 2000s, AI became more **interactive and intelligent**:

- ITS could assess student responses and adapt instructions accordingly.
- Systems like Carnegie Learning for math or AutoTutor for science began to mimic human tutoring styles.
- Early AI could track student mistakes, suggest corrections, and adjust difficulty levels.

Teachers began to **share instructional roles** with AI, though still in a supportive manner.

3. The Online Learning Revolution

The rise of MOOCs (Massive Open Online Courses) and digital platforms accelerated AI integration:

- AI helped with **personalized course recommendations** and learning path suggestions.
- Natural Language Processing (NLP) enabled smart grading of essays and language inputs.
- AI-driven chatbots answered student queries and offered basic administrative support.

AI became a **bridge between students and teachers**, offering 24/7 guidance and support.

4. The GenAI Leap: Co-Creation and Co-Teaching

With the emergence of **Generative AI**, we are witnessing a new era of **human-AI collaboration**:

- AI is no longer just executing commands; it is **co-creating** content, simulations, quizzes, and personalized materials.
- Teachers use GenAI to generate diverse examples, analogies, and multilingual explanations.

- GenAI can **co-teach** by providing one-on-one student support, freeing teachers for high-touch, creative engagement.

Teachers and AI function as **co-educators**, each focusing on their strengths—human empathy and AI scalability.

5. Teachers as Designers, Curators, and Mentors

In AI-augmented classrooms:

- Teachers curate and refine AI-generated content to fit learners' contexts.
- They monitor AI feedback and step in when emotional intelligence is needed.
- Educators design assessments and projects that **go beyond AI's reach**, focusing on creativity, ethics, and critical thinking.

Teachers evolve into **learning architects**, shaping experiences instead of just delivering content.

6. Students as Co-Explorers with AI

Students now engage with GenAI as:

- Learning companions (e.g., brainstorming with ChatGPT, solving problems with AI tutors)
- Feedback engines (getting real-time input on essays, pronunciation, or code)
- Creative partners (generating stories, presentations, or simulations)

This fosters **self-directed learning, exploration, and confidence**.

7. Responsible Collaboration: Guardrails and Ethics

While the benefits are immense, collaborative use of AI in education requires:

- **Transparency**: Making AI's role in grading or content generation clear
- **Ethics**: Teaching students how to use AI responsibly and avoid over-reliance
- **Bias Mitigation**: Ensuring AI systems are fair and inclusive
- **Teacher Oversight**: Human judgment remains central in decision-making

The Future: A Harmonious Human-AI Ecosystem

The ultimate goal is not for AI to replace human roles, but to **enhance them**.

In the evolving educational landscape, **teachers are empowered, students are engaged, and AI is the silent but powerful partner** —working behind the scenes to elevate the learning experience.

The future classroom is not about choosing between human or AI. It's about building a **collaborative, compassionate, and intelligent alliance** that brings out the best in both.

CASE STUDIES FROM K–12 SCHOOLS, COLLEGES, AND UNIVERSITIES

Generative AI has already started reshaping education across various levels and regions. Below are real-life success stories that highlight how GenAI is transforming classrooms—from kindergarten to university—by personalizing learning, enhancing creativity, reducing teacher workload, and bridging educational gaps.

Case Study 1: K–12 — Personalized Learning at Scale in the USA

School: *Montgomery County Public Schools, Maryland*
Tool Used: *Khanmigo (Khan Academy + GPT-4)*

Montgomery County integrated Khanmigo as a virtual tutor and coach to support student learning in math and science.

Impact:

- Students received **real-time explanations** on math problems.
- The tool adjusted the **difficulty level based on student performance**.
- Teachers used Khanmigo to analyze where students struggled, enabling **targeted intervention**.

Result: Increased math scores and greater student confidence, especially among underperforming groups.

Case Study 2: K–12 — AI Writing Companion in the UK

School: *Outwood Grange Academies Trust*
Tool Used: *MagicSchool AI + ChatGPT*

The school deployed GenAI tools to assist students in **developing writing skills** and reduce teacher burden for assignment feedback.

Impact:

- Students used AI to brainstorm ideas, get grammar suggestions, and improve vocabulary.
- Teachers focused more on **creativity and idea development**, rather than mechanical editing.

Result: Improved essay quality and **enhanced engagement** with writing tasks.

Case Study 3: College — AI-Powered Course Content at Arizona State University (ASU)

Institution: *ASU + OpenAI Collaboration*
Tool Used: *Custom GPTs for course design and tutoring*

ASU introduced GenAI to help students and faculty across departments:

Impact:

- Professors used GPT to **generate quiz questions, summaries, and slides**.
- Students accessed 24/7 tutoring on coding, calculus, and writing.

Result: Reduced prep time for faculty and **greater academic support** for students.

Case Study 4: University — Multilingual Support in India's

Higher Education

Institution: *Indian Institute of Technology (IIT) Delhi*
Tool Used: *Bhashini + GPT-based AI Translation Tools*

AI-powered tools helped translate complex STEM course materials into **regional languages** like Hindi, Tamil, and Bengali.

Impact:

- Students from rural areas could understand **engineering and science topics** better.
- Faculty reached a **wider audience** using multilingual GenAI content.

Result: Boosted inclusivity and **reduced dropout rates** in remote areas.

Case Study 5: Global — Special Education Support in Australia

School: *Sydney Catholic Schools Network*
Tool Used: *Curipod + GPT-4 Accessibility Enhancements*

GenAI created tailored lesson plans and visual aids for students with learning disabilities (dyslexia, ADHD, autism).

Impact:

- AI offered **multi-modal content**—audio, visual, simplified text.
- Teachers collaborated with AI to build **individual learning journeys**.

Result: Improved engagement and performance in **neurodiverse learners**.

Case Study 6: GenAI for Creativity — Parsons School of Design, New York

Department: *Fashion & Graphic Design*
Tool Used: *DALL·E, Midjourney + ChatGPT for creative prompts*

Students and faculty used GenAI to **prototype visual concepts** and **co-create designs** with AI input.

Impact:

- Accelerated ideation processes.
- Students learned to **collaborate with AI creatively**, not just analytically.

Result: A surge in **innovation, speed, and originality** in student work.

Key Takeaways

Impact Area	Outcome
Personalization	Custom learning paths and real-time tutoring
Inclusion	Multilingual, adaptive, and disability-friendly content
Teacher Empowerment	Reduced workload and AI-generated resources
Creative Enhancement	AI-assisted brainstorming, design, and multimedia integration
Academic Performance Boost	Increased engagement and improvement in grades

GLOBAL PERSPECTIVES: HOW GENAI IS TRANSFORMING EDUCATION WORLDWIDE

Generative AI (GenAI) is reshaping the education landscape across continents, providing solutions to diverse challenges, from accessibility and personalization to teacher empowerment and curriculum development. Below is a curated look at how various countries are adopting GenAI in education.

United States — Personalized Tutoring at Scale

Tool: *Khanmigo (Khan Academy + GPT-4)*
Use Case: Nationwide trials in K–12 education

- Provides **AI-driven personalized tutoring** in real time.
- Students engage with Socratic questioning and adaptive learning paths.
- Teachers gain insights into learning gaps through AI dashboards.

Result: Boosted math scores, better engagement, and efficient intervention.

China — AI Teachers in Smart Classrooms

Tool: *Squirrel AI + AI Writing Assistants*
Use Case: AI instructors deployed in both urban and rural schools

- Delivers **adaptive lessons and practice exercises** based on each student's pace.
- AI handles repetitive grading and content delivery.

Result: More time for teachers to focus on mentoring; improved outcomes in math and science.

United Kingdom — Reducing Teacher Workload

Tool: *MagicSchool AI, TeachMateAI, ChatGPT*
Use Case: AI tools supporting lesson planning and marking

- Teachers generate **lesson plans, report comments, and resources** in minutes.
- Integrated GenAI assistants help with content differentiation for mixed-ability classrooms.

Result: Time savings of up to 10 hours per week per teacher; improved job satisfaction.

India — Language Inclusion & Rural Access

Tool: *Bhashini AI + GPT-based Translators*
Use Case: Translating higher education materials into regional languages

- STEM and professional course materials translated in real time.
- AI chatbots support 24/7 learning in rural areas.

Result: Reduced dropout rates, increased access for non-English speakers, and stronger rural participation.

Australia — Inclusive Learning for Neurodiverse Students

Tool: *Curipod + ChatGPT for Accessibility*
Use Case: Special education needs in primary and secondary schools

- Multi-sensory AI-generated content tailored for ADHD, dyslexia, and autism.
- Teachers collaborate with AI to create **individualized learning plans (ILPs).**

Result: Enhanced learning engagement and inclusion across neurodiverse classrooms.

France — AI for Baccalauréat Preparation

Tool: *OpenAI models + Local AI platforms*
Use Case: Assisting students in national exam preparation

- AI chatbots offer structured revision plans, instant explanations, and mock tests.
- Available via mobile apps for low-bandwidth access.

Result: Improved confidence and performance in high-stakes exams like the Baccalauréat.

Brazil — Closing the Urban-Rural Gap

Tool: *GenAI mobile apps + WhatsApp-based Learning Bots*
Use Case: Delivering education to underserved communities

- AI supports **offline learning**, voice-based feedback, and mobile-first lesson delivery.
- GenAI writes bilingual content and lesson plans for community teachers.

Result: Better literacy rates and foundational numeracy among first-gen learners.

Singapore — GenAI for Teacher Training and Upskilling

Tool: *AI-embedded LMS (Learning Management Systems)*
Use Case: National-level teacher training programs

- GenAI provides personalized professional development paths.
- AI analyzes teaching styles and recommends pedagogical improvements.

Result: Stronger teacher confidence in digital tools and AI integration.

Key Global Impacts of GenAI in Education

Country	Focus Area	Outcome
USA	Personalized Tutoring	Higher scores and learning efficiency
China	Smart Classrooms	Scalable education in rural + urban settings
UK	Teacher Workload Reduction	Less burnout, more creativity
India	Language & Rural Access	Inclusion of millions of regional learners
Australia	Special Needs Education	Engagement for neurodiverse learners
France	National Exam Support	Better preparation and performance
Brazil	Rural and Low-Income Students	Literacy and access gains
Singapore	Teacher Upskilling with GenAI	Professional growth and future-readiness

LESSONS LEARNED FROM EARLY ADOPTERS AND VISIONARIES

As schools and universities begin to integrate Generative AI (GenAI) into their ecosystems, early adopters offer powerful insights into what works, what doesn't, and what the future could look like. These pioneers—educators, institutions, technologists, and policymakers—have illuminated a new path in teaching and learning. Below are the key lessons learned from their journeys:

1. Start Small, Scale Fast

Case Insight:
A California charter school began with a pilot using GenAI for personalized reading support in two 5th-grade classrooms. After seeing a 20% improvement in comprehension levels within a semester, they expanded school-wide the following year.

Lesson:
Begin with focused, measurable pilots before scaling. This reduces resistance and builds confidence through quick wins.

2. Teacher Involvement is Critical

Case Insight:
In Finland, AI-powered learning systems were co-developed **with teachers** through feedback loops. Educators were trained in prompt engineering, scenario testing, and classroom integration strategies.

Lesson:
Involve teachers from the beginning—not just as users, but as co-creators. Their insights ensure relevance and increase adoption.

3. Customization Over One-Size-Fits-All

Case Insight:
A South Korean university used GenAI to offer **customized feedback** on writing assignments across departments. The system adapted to subject-specific styles—engineering reports vs. literature essays.

Lesson:
GenAI is most effective when tailored to content domain and learner context. Avoid generic implementations.

4. Privacy and Ethics Cannot Be Afterthoughts

Case Insight:
A Canadian school board faced backlash when parents discovered AI tools logging sensitive student data. After public scrutiny, the board overhauled its privacy practices and implemented **ethical AI policies**.

Lesson:
Transparency and data protection build trust. Always embed privacy-by-design and obtain stakeholder consent.

5. Local Language and Cultural Context Matter

Case Insight:
In Kenya, an edtech startup trained GenAI tools on Swahili and

local proverbs to improve literacy outcomes. Students related better to culturally relevant content.

Lesson:
Localize AI tools to language, culture, and curriculum for deeper engagement and stronger learning outcomes.

6. Measure What Matters

Case Insight:
A UK college set clear KPIs: student satisfaction, teacher workload, and performance improvement. Their GenAI dashboard allowed them to iterate quickly.

Lesson:
Define success metrics early and monitor regularly. Let the data guide optimization and scaling decisions.

7. Partnerships with AI Companies Accelerate Growth

Case Insight:
An Indian state partnered with an AI startup and UNESCO to deploy multilingual GenAI chatbots across 10,000 government schools.

Lesson:
Public-private partnerships can bring resources, speed, and innovation—especially in under-resourced areas.

8. Student Voice Enhances Adoption

Case Insight:
At a New York high school, students helped design prompts for their AI tutors. This gamified learning and encouraged ownership.

Lesson:
Let students co-create and interact with AI. They are digital natives and often the most innovative users.

9. Leadership Vision Drives Transformation

Case Insight:
A Singapore school principal led GenAI integration through a 3-year vision plan, involving staff retraining, curriculum redesign, and regular community updates.

Lesson:
Visionary leadership is vital. Change requires strategy, storytelling, and stamina.

10. AI is a Tool, Not a Replacement

Case Insight:
In Brazil, AI was initially perceived as a threat to teachers. But when reframed as a **"co-teacher"** handling grading, lesson planning, and admin tasks, resistance faded.

Lesson:
Position AI as an **augmentation**, not a substitution. It's here to empower, not replace, educators.

Conclusion: The Road Ahead

The lessons from these early adopters make one thing clear —GenAI is not a silver bullet, but a **powerful catalyst** when deployed thoughtfully. With human-AI collaboration, empathy-driven design, and equitable policies, we can redefine education for generations to come.

THE ETHICS OF AI
IN EDUCATION

As Generative AI (GenAI) becomes increasingly embedded in educational systems, it brings immense opportunities—but also serious ethical challenges. The integration of AI into classrooms isn't just a technological shift; it's a **moral responsibility**. Addressing ethical concerns is essential to ensure fairness, privacy, inclusivity, and trust in education systems powered by AI.

1. Bias and Fairness

Challenge:
AI algorithms learn from data, and if that data reflects historical inequalities—such as racial, gender, or socio-economic bias—AI may **reinforce or even amplify discrimination**.

Example:
If a grading AI is trained on essays mostly from native English speakers, it may unfairly penalize students with different linguistic backgrounds.

Ethical Response:
- Use diverse and inclusive training datasets.
- Regularly audit algorithms for bias.
- Involve ethicists, teachers, and students in reviewing outcomes.

2. Data Privacy and Consent

Challenge:

AI systems require large amounts of student data (performance, behavior, biometrics) to function effectively. If mishandled, this can lead to **privacy breaches** and unauthorized surveillance.

Example:

An AI platform collecting facial recognition data for attendance could pose privacy risks if not properly secured or regulated.

Ethical Response:

- Comply with data protection laws (e.g., GDPR, FERPA).
- Obtain informed consent from students and guardians.
- Anonymize data wherever possible.

---

3. Accountability and Transparency

Challenge:

When AI systems make decisions—like grading or recommending students for gifted programs—who is responsible if something goes wrong?

Example:

If a student is unfairly flagged for academic dishonesty by an AI, they must have a way to appeal and receive human review.

Ethical Response:

- Keep human oversight in all high-stakes decisions.
- Ensure AI systems are explainable and not "black boxes."
- Establish clear accountability protocols.

---

4. Equity and Access

Challenge:

AI has the potential to widen the digital divide. Schools in under-resourced areas may lack the infrastructure or funding to benefit from GenAI tools.

Example:

A rural school without internet access cannot use AI-driven learning apps, leaving students behind.

Ethical Response:

- Design low-bandwidth and offline-compatible tools.
- Push for equitable distribution of AI resources.
- Partner with NGOs or governments to support underserved communities.

5. Student Autonomy and Freedom

Challenge:

Over-reliance on AI may reduce student independence and critical thinking. Constant guidance or recommendations from AI could lead to **over-dependence**.

Example:

If students always use AI-generated summaries instead of reading the material, deep learning suffers.

Ethical Response:

- Encourage human-AI collaboration rather than automation.
- Promote AI as a support tool, not a substitute for thinking.
- Educate students on responsible AI use.

6. Teacher Roles and Job Security

Challenge:

There's concern among educators that AI could replace human teaching roles, leading to **job insecurity or devaluation** of the teacher's role.

Example:

AI grading systems or automated lesson planners might be seen as replacements rather than aids.

Ethical Response:

- Emphasize AI as a tool for **augmentation**, not replacement.
- Invest in AI literacy and training for teachers.
- Reframe AI as a partner in teaching, enhancing creativity and emotional support.

Conclusion: Building an Ethical AI Framework in Education

To ethically harness the power of AI in education, stakeholders must focus on:

- **Transparency** in how AI tools are designed and used
- **Equity** in access to AI resources
- **Consent** and **privacy protections**
- **Bias detection and mitigation**
- **Continual human oversight and accountability**

When ethics is embedded into the design and deployment of AI in education, we don't just build smarter systems— we build **fairer, more compassionate, and inclusive learning environments**.

BIAS, FAIRNESS, AND TRANSPARENCY IN GENAI ALGORITHMS

As Generative AI (GenAI) becomes a cornerstone in modern education systems, the **integrity of its algorithms**—particularly in terms of bias, fairness, and transparency—becomes a critical concern. GenAI systems are designed to assist with personalized learning, grading, curriculum development, and more, but they also reflect the **assumptions, values, and limitations** of the data and creators behind them.

1. Understanding Bias in GenAI

Bias occurs when an AI system produces prejudiced results due to flawed data, assumptions, or models. Bias can creep into GenAI in subtle but impactful ways.

Examples of Bias in Education AI:

- **Language Bias**: A GenAI tool trained primarily on Western English texts may struggle with regional dialects or diverse cultural references.
- **Cultural Bias**: AI suggesting content may favor certain historical perspectives, ignoring marginalized voices.
- **Gender or Racial Bias**: AI might unintentionally stereotype students in performance predictions or discipline alerts.

Key Sources of Bias:

- **Training Data**: If the dataset is unbalanced or historically biased.
- **Model Design**: If developers hard-code assumptions or exclude demographic variability.
- **Feedback Loops**: If an AI's decisions reinforce and learn from existing biased outputs.

2. Promoting Fairness

Fairness in GenAI means **equal opportunity and treatment** for all students, regardless of background, ability, or geography.

Strategies to Enhance Fairness:

- **Inclusive Dataset Curation**: Include data from diverse schools, regions, learning styles, and languages.
- **Representation Audits**: Routinely test AI outputs across different demographics to spot disparities.
- **Context-Aware Design**: Consider socioeconomic, cultural, and linguistic contexts in GenAI's educational recommendations.

Fairness is not just about equal treatment but also **equitable support**—tailoring resources to meet different learners' needs.

3. Ensuring Transparency

Transparency is about **making the workings of GenAI systems understandable and open**—to educators, students, and parents.

Why Transparency Matters:

- **Builds Trust**: Teachers and students are more likely to adopt GenAI tools they can understand.
- **Enables Accountability**: Clear AI processes make it easier to correct errors or challenge unfair outcomes.
- **Supports Ethics**: Transparent systems reduce the risk of "black box" decisions that no one can explain.

Tools for Transparency:

- **Explainable AI (XAI)**: Models that offer reasons for their decisions (e.g., why a student got a certain score).
- **Documentation and Open Models**: Sharing how an algorithm was trained, its limitations, and its intended use.
- **Human-in-the-Loop Systems**: Ensure educators can review and override GenAI decisions when necessary.

The Risks of Opaque Systems

Without attention to bias, fairness, and transparency, GenAI systems can:

- **Disadvantage underrepresented students**
- **Widen existing achievement gaps**
- **Cause psychological harm or mistrust in AI tools**
- **Erode public confidence in AI-enhanced education**

Final Thought

For GenAI to truly **redefine education in a just and inclusive way**, we must embed principles of **bias mitigation, fairness, and transparency** into every phase of development and deployment. This is not a one-time task—it is a continuous commitment to **ethical, human-centered AI**.

THE IMPORTANCE OF HUMAN-CENTERED AI DESIGN

As AI—especially Generative AI (GenAI)—becomes deeply integrated into education, it's vital that these systems are designed with **humans at the core**, not just as end-users, but as **co-creators, decision-makers, and beneficiaries**. Human-centered AI design ensures that technological solutions are **ethical, empathetic, and truly empowering**.

What is Human-Centered AI Design?

Human-centered AI design is a framework that prioritizes the **needs, values, emotions, and experiences of people** throughout the AI development process. In education, this means designing GenAI tools that:

- Understand diverse learners' needs
- Support rather than replace educators
- Respect cultural, social, and emotional contexts
- Are transparent, accessible, and inclusive

Key Principles of Human-Centered AI in Education

1. Empathy-Driven Design

- Understand students' and teachers' daily challenges.
- Build tools that solve real classroom problems, not

hypothetical ones.

- Include emotional intelligence (EQ) to recognize stress, motivation, or disengagement.

2. Inclusivity and Accessibility

- Design for students with disabilities (e.g., text-to-speech, visual aids).
- Support multiple languages, learning styles, and levels of digital literacy.
- Ensure AI doesn't alienate underprivileged or marginalized groups.

3. Teacher-AI Collaboration

- GenAI should act as a **teaching assistant**, not a replacement.
- Allow teachers to customize AI recommendations based on classroom dynamics.
- Provide teachers with insights, not mandates.

4. Transparency and Explainability

- Clearly show how and why AI reaches decisions (e.g., student performance scores).
- Empower users to question or override AI suggestions.
- Reduce the "black box" problem of opaque algorithms.

5. Feedback-First Iteration

- Involve educators and students in the design and testing process.
- Continuously refine tools based on real-world use and feedback.
- Encourage co-creation, not top-down development.

Why Human-Centered Design Matters in Education

Supports Holistic Learning

AI can optimize curriculum and assessment, but **only humans can nurture creativity, emotional resilience, and ethical reasoning.**

Respects Human Agency

When GenAI systems are designed around people, they reinforce autonomy rather than control or manipulate behavior.

Enhances Engagement and Outcomes

Students and educators engage more with tools that feel **intuitive, empathetic, and helpful**, improving educational outcomes.

Minimizes Harm

A human-centered approach helps **prevent harm** like over-surveillance, biased feedback, or depersonalized education.

Moving Forward: Designing for Human Impact

The future of AI in education isn't about creating **super-intelligent systems**—it's about creating **super-useful systems** that help people thrive.

Human-centered GenAI must:

- **Empower, not overpower**
- **Collaborate, not dictate**
- **Inspire, not standardize**

PREPARING STUDENTS FOR A WORLD WITH GENAI

As Generative AI (GenAI) becomes more embedded in daily life—transforming industries, redefining careers, and reshaping the way we learn and think—it's crucial that **students are not only users of GenAI but also informed participants, creators, and critics** of this technology.

Preparing students for a GenAI-powered world means cultivating both **technical fluency and ethical awareness**, while nurturing human skills that machines cannot replicate.

Key Goals of GenAI-Ready Education

1. Digital Literacy → AI Literacy

Students must go beyond basic digital skills to understand:

- What GenAI is and how it works (conceptually)
- Its capabilities and limitations
- How to critically evaluate AI-generated content
- Responsible use of AI tools in academics and life

2. Encouraging Creative & Critical Thinking

While GenAI can generate ideas and content, students must:

- Analyze and critique AI outputs
- Build on them creatively

- Learn to question, refine, and personalize content

This promotes **active learning**, not passive consumption.

3. Ethics and Responsible Use

Students should be taught:

- The ethics of AI in decision-making
- How to spot misinformation or AI-generated bias
- When and how to disclose AI use (e.g., in writing or projects)
- The importance of human judgment alongside AI tools

4. Collaboration with AI

Train students to see AI as a **partner**, not a replacement:

- Use GenAI for brainstorming, tutoring, simulations
- Learn co-working strategies: prompt design, iteration, evaluation
- Develop human-AI collaboration skills (a growing workforce demand)

5. Human Skills Remain Essential

As GenAI handles routine tasks, students need to focus on:

- Emotional intelligence (EQ)
- Empathy, ethics, and leadership
- Interpersonal communication
- Cultural competence and adaptability

These are the skills that will **differentiate humans in an AI-driven world**.

Practical Ways to Prepare Students

1. Integrate GenAI into Curriculum

- Use GenAI in research, writing, and coding assignments

- Teach prompt engineering and tool evaluation
- Design "AI + Human" group projects

2. Offer AI Ethics & Awareness Modules

- Use real-world case studies
- Debate AI dilemmas (e.g., surveillance vs. safety, plagiarism vs. creativity)
- Teach how AI impacts privacy, jobs, justice

3. Hands-On Experience

- Let students experiment with GenAI platforms like ChatGPT, DALL·E, or code-generating tools
- Build small AI projects or simulations
- Encourage safe exploration with teacher guidance

4. Career & Future Readiness

- Connect AI skills with future careers
- Invite experts or industry mentors to speak about AI in their field
- Showcase interdisciplinary GenAI use (e.g., in art, medicine, business, climate)

Final Thought

Preparing students for a GenAI world is about more than technology—it's about shaping **ethical, adaptable, and curious minds**. The classroom must evolve into a space where students learn to harness AI while staying deeply human in their values, creativity, and purpose.

THE BENEFITS OF A GENAI-POWERED EDUCATIONAL SYSTEM

A GenAI-powered educational system isn't just about automation or digital tools—it's about **transforming how students learn, how teachers teach, and how educational institutions operate**. By integrating Generative AI into the core of learning experiences, we unlock a more inclusive, efficient, and personalized education system for all.

1. Personalized Learning at Scale

GenAI can adapt content, pace, and assessments to suit the **individual learning style and progress** of each student:

- Automatically recommends resources tailored to student needs.
- Adjusts difficulty levels based on real-time performance.
- Supports diverse learners with multilingual and multimedia content.

Example: A student struggling with algebra receives simpler explanations, additional visual aids, and practice problems generated on the fly.

2. 24/7 Intelligent Tutoring

GenAI can act as a **round-the-clock tutor**, providing instant answers, clarifications, and feedback:

- Helps with homework, test prep, and concepts.
- Encourages independent learning and curiosity.
- Reduces students' reliance on classroom time alone.

Example: A student preparing for exams at midnight uses GenAI to quiz themselves and get feedback instantly.

3. Real-Time Feedback and Continuous Assessment

Rather than waiting for exam results, GenAI can:

- Offer **instant feedback** on written work, quizzes, and projects.
- Help students improve through **iterative learning loops**.
- Enable teachers to focus on higher-order feedback and mentoring.

Example: An essay is evaluated for structure, grammar, and logic with AI suggestions on how to improve.

4. Empowering Educators

GenAI supports teachers by:

- Automating repetitive tasks like grading and lesson planning.
- Providing insights on student progress and learning gaps.
- Suggesting instructional strategies and materials.

Result: Teachers have more time to focus on **emotional engagement, creativity, and personalized mentoring**.

5. Enhanced Engagement and Interactivity

GenAI can make learning more engaging through:

- Interactive storytelling
- AI-powered simulations
- Personalized learning games and quizzes

Example: History lessons transformed into choose-your-own-adventure AI experiences.

6. Accessibility and Inclusion

GenAI can bridge learning gaps for:

- Students with disabilities (text-to-speech, voice input, image recognition)
- Non-native language speakers (automatic translation)
- Remote or underserved communities (AI-powered offline content)

Example: A visually impaired student uses an AI tool that reads aloud and describes diagrams in real time.

7. Scalability and Cost Efficiency

Once deployed, GenAI systems can serve **millions of students simultaneously**, without proportional increases in cost:

- Ideal for large or under-resourced educational institutions.
- Can be implemented in mobile apps, websites, or offline devices.

8. Data-Driven Decision Making

GenAI can analyze vast educational data to:

- Identify patterns and learning bottlenecks.
- Forecast academic outcomes.
- Inform policy, curriculum updates, and teaching

strategies.

9. Fostering Lifelong Learning

GenAI enables **self-paced, interest-driven learning** beyond the classroom:

- Adult learners can reskill and upskill using personalized GenAI coaches.
- Learners can pursue interdisciplinary knowledge with AI guidance.

10. Future-Ready Skills Development

GenAI not only teaches academic subjects but also promotes:

- Digital fluency and AI literacy
- Critical thinking about technology
- Ethical understanding of AI use in life and work

Final Thought

A GenAI-powered educational system isn't just an upgrade— it's a **paradigm shift** that makes learning more **human-centric, inclusive, and forward-looking**. It's about building a smarter system that empowers every learner and educator to thrive in the 21st century and beyond.

CASE STUDY: PERSONALIZED LEARNING ASSISTANT FOR MIDDLE SCHOOL MATH STUDENTS

Objective:

To improve math performance for middle school students by using a GenAI-powered chatbot that provides personalized practice, explanations, and feedback based on student responses.

Background:

Sunrise Valley School, a mid-sized school in India, implemented a GenAI chatbot in their 7th-grade math classes. The goal was to assist students in solving algebra problems and clarify their doubts outside classroom hours.

Implementation:

- A chatbot was built using OpenAI's GPT model.
- The chatbot could:
    - Ask math questions tailored to student performance.
    - Provide step-by-step feedback.
    - Offer hints, explanations, and encouragement.

Results:

After 3 months:

- 87% of students reported better understanding.
- Teachers saw a 35% improvement in quiz scores.
- Students spent more time practicing math at home.

Sample Code: GenAI-Powered Math Tutor (Using OpenAI GPT API)

This is a Python-based example that simulates a personalized math tutor.

```python
import openai

# Set your OpenAI API key
openai.api_key = "your-api-key-here"

def ask_gpt(prompt):
    response = openai.ChatCompletion.create(
        model="gpt-4", # or "gpt-3.5-turbo"
        messages=[
            {"role": "system", "content": "You are a helpful math tutor for 7th-grade students."},
            {"role": "user", "content": prompt}
        ],
        temperature=0.7,
        max_tokens=500
    )
    return response.choices[0].message["content"].strip()

# Example session with the AI tutor
```

```
student_question = "Can you help me understand how to solve
2x + 3 = 11?"

response = ask_gpt(student_question)

print("AI Tutor:", response)
```

Example Output:

AI Tutor: Sure! Let's solve the equation 2x + 3 = 11 step by step.

Step 1: Subtract 3 from both sides:

2x + 3 - 3 = 11 - 3

=> 2x = 8

Step 2: Divide both sides by 2:

2x / 2 = 8 / 2

=> x = 4

So, the solution is x = 4.

Extensions You Can Add:

- Track student performance over time.
- Use a database to store questions and student answers.
- Add a frontend using Flask or Streamlit for web-based interface.

CASE STUDY: AI WRITING ASSISTANT FOR ESSAY FEEDBACK IN HIGH SCHOOL

Objective:

To enhance students' writing skills by using a GenAI-based assistant that provides real-time feedback on grammar, coherence, tone, and structure.

Background:

Starlight High School in Bengaluru introduced an AI-powered writing tool in English classes for Grades 9 and 10. The tool used GenAI (GPT-4) to review essays and offer constructive suggestions within seconds.

Implementation:

- Teachers integrated the assistant into the school's learning portal.
- Students uploaded their essays or typed directly into the interface.
- GenAI provided:
    - Grammar and spelling corrections.
    - Suggestions for clearer structure and improved arguments.

◦ Feedback on tone and style.

Results:

- 40% improvement in writing scores across 2 terms.
- Students revised their essays 2.3x more on average.
- Teachers saved hours on repetitive feedback.

Python Code: GenAI Essay Reviewer using OpenAI

This script takes an essay input and uses GPT-4 to return writing feedback.

```python
import openai

# Set your OpenAI API key
openai.api_key = "your-api-key-here"

def review_essay(essay_text):
    prompt = f"""
You are an English language teacher. Read the following student essay and provide:
- Overall feedback
- Suggestions to improve clarity, grammar, tone, and structure.
- Highlight strengths and areas to improve.

Essay:
\"\"\"{essay_text}\"\"\"
"""

    response = openai.ChatCompletion.create(
        model="gpt-4",
```

```python
    messages=[
        {"role": "system", "content": "You are a helpful and
encouraging writing assistant."},
        {"role": "user", "content": prompt}
    ],
    temperature=0.6,
    max_tokens=700
)
    return response.choices[0].message["content"].strip()

# Sample essay for feedback
student_essay = """
```

Technology has made our lives easier, but it also come with many problems. People are now addicted to phones and social media, and they are not spending time in real life. Also, it is causing health problems.

```
"""

# Get feedback
feedback = review_essay(student_essay)
print("AI Feedback:\n", feedback)
```

Sample Output:

AI Feedback:

Your essay brings up a relevant and important topic. Here's my feedback:

Strengths:

- You clearly identify a main idea and support it with examples.

- The language is easy to understand.

Suggestions:

- Correct "come" to "comes" for grammatical accuracy.

- Expand your arguments with examples (e.g., how social media affects health).

- Use transitions to improve the flow between ideas.

- Consider adding a concluding sentence.

Overall, you're on the right track. Keep writing and revising!

Extensions You Could Add:

- Track writing improvement across multiple essays.
- Enable voice-to-text input for accessibility.
- Allow teachers to comment or approve feedback.

CASE STUDY: VIRTUAL SCIENCE LAB ASSISTANT FOR HIGH SCHOOL PHYSICS

Objective:

To enable interactive, AI-guided lab simulations and explanations for students who lack access to physical science lab equipment—especially during online or hybrid learning setups.

Background:

Harmony Public School, located in a rural district, introduced a GenAI-based virtual lab assistant in its Grade 11 Physics class. Due to funding limitations, the school couldn't afford full lab infrastructure.

Students used the assistant to:

- Simulate experiments (like Newton's Laws, projectile motion).
- Ask questions and receive visual or stepwise explanations.
- Practice solving lab-based questions and generate reports.

Implementation:

- Students accessed the assistant via a simple web app.
- AI generated detailed responses and simulated results.
- Integrated ChatGPT-style interaction tailored for science learners.

Results:

- 90% engagement increase in Physics lab hours.
- 70% of students reported stronger conceptual understanding.
- Improved practical scores by 40% in the term exams.

Python Code: Virtual Physics Lab Assistant Using GenAI

This example simulates a conversation with an AI lab assistant that explains a physics concept or experiment.

```python
import openai

# Set your OpenAI API key
openai.api_key = "your-api-key-here"

def physics_lab_assistant(query):
    prompt = f"""
```

You are a Physics lab assistant. A high school student asks the following question related to a Physics experiment or concept.

Provide a step-by-step explanation, simulate outcomes if applicable, and encourage the student to think critically.

Student's Question:
{query}
"""

```
response = openai.ChatCompletion.create(
    model="gpt-4",
    messages=[
        {"role": "system", "content": "You are a knowledgeable
and friendly physics lab assistant."},
        {"role": "user", "content": prompt}
    ],
    temperature=0.5,
    max_tokens=600
)
return response.choices[0].message["content"].strip()

# Example use
student_query = "Can you explain how projectile motion works
and show a sample calculation?"
response = physics_lab_assistant(student_query)
print("AI Lab Assistant:\n", response)
```

Example Output:

AI Lab Assistant:

Sure! Projectile motion is a form of motion where an object moves in a curved path under the influence of gravity alone (assuming air resistance is negligible).

Let's say we launch a ball with an initial velocity of 20 m/s at a 45° angle.

Step 1: Break velocity into components:

- Horizontal (Vx) = 20 * cos(45°) ≈ 14.14 m/s
- Vertical (Vy) = 20 * sin(45°) ≈ 14.14 m/s

Step 2: Time of flight:

T = 2 * Vy / g ≈ 2 * 14.14 / 9.8 ≈ 2.88 s

Step 3: Range:

R = Vx * T ≈ 14.14 * 2.88 ≈ 40.74 meters

So, the ball will land approximately 40.74 meters away.

Would you like to simulate with different angles or speeds?

Expandable Features:

- Add visual simulation using Python libraries like matplotlib.
- Store student Q&A history for progress analysis.
- Integrate into a school's LMS (Learning Management System).

CASE STUDY: GENAI-POWERED LANGUAGE TUTOR FOR ESL STUDENTS

Objective:

To provide personalized English language tutoring for non-native speakers, with real-time correction, vocabulary building, and pronunciation support.

Background:

Bright Minds Academy in Gujarat implemented a GenAI-based language assistant for students from rural areas who had limited exposure to conversational English. Traditional classroom methods weren't enough to build confidence in speaking and writing fluency.

The GenAI system provided:

- Daily language practice tasks.
- Real-time grammar corrections.
- Conversational simulations.
- Vocabulary and idiom explanations in native languages (Gujarati, Hindi).

Results:

- 55% improvement in spoken English fluency (as per assessments).
- Increased classroom participation.
- Parents reported better confidence in children when interacting in public.

Python Code: ESL Tutor Using GenAI (Grammar & Vocabulary Assistant)

This assistant corrects grammar and explains vocabulary in simple terms.

import openai

Set your OpenAI API key

openai.api_key = "your-api-key-here"

def esl_tutor(student_input, native_language="Hindi"):

prompt = f"""

You are an AI English tutor helping a student who is learning English as a second language.

The student's native language is {native_language}.

1. Correct the grammar and spelling in the student's sentence.

2. Explain any difficult words in simple English and in {native_language}.

3. Suggest a better way to say the sentence naturally in spoken English.

Student's input:

"{student_input}"

"""

```python
response = openai.ChatCompletion.create(
    model="gpt-4",
    messages=[
        {"role": "system", "content": "You are a friendly and encouraging ESL teacher."},
        {"role": "user", "content": prompt}
    ],
    temperature=0.5,
    max_tokens=600
)
return response.choices[0].message["content"].strip()

# Example ESL query
student_sentence = "Yesterday I go to market and buyed many fruit."
output = esl_tutor(student_sentence)
print("AI ESL Tutor:\n", output)
```

Example Output:

AI ESL Tutor:

Corrected Sentence:

"Yesterday, I went to the market and bought many fruits."

Vocabulary Help:

- "Bought" means past tense of "buy" (खरीदा).

- "Fruits" are sweet food items that grow on trees or plants (फल).

Natural English Version:

"Yesterday, I went shopping at the market and picked up a lot of fruit."

Keep practicing! You're doing great

Bonus Ideas:

- Add pronunciation support using gTTS or pyttsx3.
- Use voice input with speech_recognition for listening practice.
- Allow quizzes and vocabulary games.

Case Study: GenAI-Powered Math Assistant for Middle School Students

Objective:

To help students grasp core math concepts such as algebra, geometry, and arithmetic through personalized AI-driven support, especially for those struggling with traditional classroom instruction.

Background:

Sunrise Learning School in Uttar Pradesh implemented a GenAI-powered math assistant for students in grades 6–8. The platform allowed students to input math problems and get step-by-step explanations.

Key Features:

- Stepwise problem breakdown.
- Error checking and concept suggestions.
- Interactive hints before giving answers.

- Visual representation using Python for geometry.

Results:

- 65% of students showed better performance in math assessments.
- 75% improvement in homework submission quality.
- Increased student confidence and reduced math anxiety.

Python Code: Math Problem Solver with Step-by-Step Explanation

This uses GenAI to solve a math problem, explain the steps, and offer guidance for learning.

```
import openai

# Set your OpenAI API key
openai.api_key = "your-api-key-here"

def math_helper(problem):
    prompt = f"""
```

You are a helpful AI math tutor. A student has asked the following math question:

"{problem}"

Please solve the problem step by step. Explain each step clearly so the student can learn the concept behind it.

Avoid giving just the final answer—focus on teaching.
```
"""
```

```
    response = openai.ChatCompletion.create(
```

```
        model="gpt-4",
        messages=[
            {"role": "system", "content": "You are a kind and patient
math tutor who helps students learn by explaining every step."},
            {"role": "user", "content": prompt}
        ],
        temperature=0.4,
        max_tokens=700
    )
    return response.choices[0].message["content"].strip()

# Example problem
problem_input = "Solve 2x + 5 = 15"
output = math_helper(problem_input)
print("AI Math Assistant:\n", output)
```

Example Output:

AI Math Assistant:

Let's solve the equation step by step:
2x + 5 = 15

Step 1: Subtract 5 from both sides
→ 2x + 5 - 5 = 15 - 5
→ 2x = 10

Step 2: Divide both sides by 2
→ 2x / 2 = 10 / 2
→ x = 5

Final Answer: x = 5

Why this works:

We isolated the variable 'x' by undoing the operations (addition and multiplication) in reverse order.

Would you like to try a similar problem next?

Possible Add-Ons:

- Visual explanations using matplotlib for graph-based problems.
- Quiz mode with hints and scoring.
- Integration with platforms like Google Classroom.

CASE STUDY: GENAI AS A RESEARCH ASSISTANT IN HIGHER EDUCATION

Objective:

To aid undergraduate and postgraduate students in academic writing, literature reviews, and research formatting using GenAI-powered guidance.

Background:

A prominent university in Delhi adopted a GenAI platform named **"ScholarMate"** to assist students struggling with writing research papers and thesis content. Students often faced difficulties in:

- Drafting well-structured literature reviews
- Citing academic sources correctly
- Understanding complex terminology
- Formulating arguments and conclusions

How It Worked:

- Students entered their topic or abstract.
- GenAI offered topic refinement, created an outline, suggested references, and helped with grammar.

- The system gave contextual recommendations and plagiarism-safe phrasing.

Results:

- 40% improvement in academic paper quality (as per faculty feedback).
- Time spent on writing reduced by 30–50%.
- Increased submission rate of research assignments and proposals.

Python Code: Academic Writing Assistant Using GenAI

This tool helps generate an academic introduction section based on a given topic.

```
import openai

# Set your OpenAI API key
openai.api_key = "your-api-key-here"

def academic_writing_assistant(topic, level="postgraduate"):
    prompt = f"""
```

You are an academic writing assistant helping a {level} student.

Generate an academic-style introduction (approx. 250 words) for a research paper on the topic:

"{topic}"

Ensure the tone is formal, includes citations placeholders (e.g., [1]), and ends with a research objective.

```
"""
```

```python
response = openai.ChatCompletion.create(
    model="gpt-4",
    messages=[
        {"role": "system", "content": "You are an expert academic writing assistant with a focus on research-level papers."},
        {"role": "user", "content": prompt}
    ],
    temperature=0.4,
    max_tokens=600
)
return response.choices[0].message["content"].strip()

# Example topic
research_topic = "The Role of Artificial Intelligence in Enhancing Cybersecurity Protocols in Higher Education Institutions"
output = academic_writing_assistant(research_topic)
print("Academic Introduction:\n", output)
```

Example Output:

Academic Introduction:

The proliferation of digital infrastructure in higher education has brought with it a corresponding increase in cybersecurity threats. Universities, as repositories of sensitive personal, academic, and financial data, are becoming prime targets for cyberattacks [1]. With the rise of remote learning and digital campuses post-pandemic, the vulnerabilities in institutional cyber defense systems have become more apparent and widespread [2].

Artificial Intelligence (AI) has emerged as a transformative technology capable of reshaping traditional cybersecurity frameworks. Through predictive analytics, automated threat detection, and real-time incident response systems, AI holds the potential to address complex and evolving cyber risks more effectively than conventional methods [3]. Notably, machine learning algorithms can identify unusual patterns of behavior, thereby enabling the early detection of breaches before they escalate [4].

Despite the growing body of literature exploring AI in cybersecurity, there remains a lack of focused research on its application within the context of higher education institutions. This paper aims to bridge that gap by evaluating the effectiveness, challenges, and ethical considerations of integrating AI-driven cybersecurity protocols in universities. The objective is to provide a comprehensive framework that institutions can adopt to bolster their cyber defenses in the age of digital academia.

Future Enhancements:

- Plagiarism checker integration.
- APA/MLA/Chicago formatting assistant.
- Recommendation system for academic journals to cite.
- Supervisor/peer feedback simulator.

CASE STUDY: GENAI IN ENGINEERING CLASSROOMS FOR REAL-TIME PROBLEM SOLVING

Objective:

To assist engineering students during lab sessions and assignments by providing **real-time GenAI-powered coding and calculation help**.

Background:

A technical institute in Bengaluru integrated a GenAI-powered assistant named **"CodeMentor AI"** in their Computer Science and Electrical Engineering departments. It was designed to:

- Help students debug code in real-time
- Explain logic and equations in simpler terms
- Offer step-by-step solutions to common algorithmic and circuit problems

---

Implementation Strategy:

- Students accessed GenAI via a chatbot embedded in the campus LMS.

- The system was trained on syllabus-specific data (Python, MATLAB, circuit theory).

- GenAI offered not just answers, but full **problem breakdowns**, **diagrams**, and **contextual explanations**.

Outcomes:

- Students reported **45% faster assignment completion**.

- **Faculty noticed higher conceptual clarity** in project submissions.

- Reduced the dropout rate in challenging core subjects by **18%**.

Python Code: GenAI-Powered Problem Solver for Physics (Kinematics Example)

This tool uses an LLM API to help students with **kinematics problems** interactively.

import openai

\# Set your OpenAI API key

openai.api_key = "your-api-key-here"

def solve_physics_problem(problem_statement):

prompt = f"""

You are a physics tutor specializing in solving kinematics problems for engineering students.

Provide a step-by-step solution with formulas and final answers for the following problem:

"{problem_statement}"

Use clear formatting and keep it academic.
"""

```python
response = openai.ChatCompletion.create(
    model="gpt-4",
    messages=[
        {"role": "system", "content": "You are a knowledgeable and patient physics tutor."},
        {"role": "user", "content": prompt}
    ],
    temperature=0.3,
    max_tokens=600
)
return response.choices[0].message["content"].strip()

# Example problem
physics_question = "A car accelerates from rest at 3 m/s² for 5 seconds. What is its final velocity and distance covered?"
solution = solve_physics_problem(physics_question)
print("Solution:\n", solution)
```

Sample Output:

Solution:

Given:

- Initial velocity, u = 0 m/s (starts from rest)

- Acceleration, a = 3 m/s²

- Time, t = 5 s

1. Final velocity (v) can be calculated using:

   v = u + at

   => v = 0 + (3 × 5) = 15 m/s

2. Distance covered (s) can be calculated using:

   $s = ut + 0.5at^2$

   => s = 0 + 0.5 × 3 × (5^2) = 0.5 × 3 × 25 = 37.5 m

Answer:

- Final Velocity: 15 m/s

- Distance Covered: 37.5 meters

Expansion Ideas:

- Add diagram generation for physics and circuit problems
- Interactive quiz mode with instant GenAI feedback
- Multi-language support for rural or international students

CASE STUDY: GENAI-POWERED LANGUAGE LAB FOR UNIVERSITY STUDENTS

Objective:

To improve proficiency in English and other foreign languages using **conversational GenAI models** for interactive speaking, writing, and comprehension practice.

Background:

A university in Kerala implemented a GenAI-based digital language lab called **"LinguaGen"**. It was integrated into their Arts & Humanities departments to help students:

- Practice spoken English and French through AI-driven conversations
- Get instant grammar and vocabulary feedback
- Translate and compare sentences between multiple languages
- Analyze tone, clarity, and fluency in writing assignments

Implementation:

- Students interacted with LinguaGen via a mobile app.

- It used **text-to-speech** and **speech-to-text** APIs alongside GenAI.
- It also supported **code-switching**, cultural context explanations, and tone detection.

Outcomes:

- **Pronunciation accuracy improved by 30%** over a semester
- **Grammar mistakes in essays reduced by 42%**
- **Student engagement in language classes increased by 60%**

Python Code: GenAI Writing & Translation Assistant

This tool helps students rewrite sentences for clarity and provides translation.

import openai

Set your OpenAI API key

openai.api_key = "your-api-key-here"

def language_helper(sentence, target_language="French"):

prompt = f"""

You are a helpful language assistant.

Given the sentence below, do the following:

1. Improve grammar and clarity.

2. Translate the improved version to {target_language}.

3. Provide a brief explanation of grammar used.

Sentence: "{sentence}"

"""

```
response = openai.ChatCompletion.create(
    model="gpt-4",
    messages=[
        {"role": "system", "content": "You are a professional linguist and language teacher."},
        {"role": "user", "content": prompt}
    ],
    temperature=0.5,
    max_tokens=700
)
return response.choices[0].message["content"].strip()

# Example usage
sentence = "He don't has no time for to learning English good."
result = language_helper(sentence, target_language="French")
print(result)
```

Sample Output:

1. Improved Sentence: "He doesn't have time to learn English well."

2. Translation (French): "Il n'a pas le temps d'apprendre l'anglais correctement."

3. Explanation:

- Corrected subject-verb agreement: "don't has" → "doesn't have"

- Removed double negative: "don't has no" → "doesn't have"

- Changed "for to learning" → "to learn"

- Replaced "good" (adj) with "well" (adv)

Future Plans:

- Add **voice-based conversation mode** with GenAI as a speaking partner
- Integration with **real-time subtitles and speech analytics**
- Personalized practice modules based on student errors